# It's Not Your
# BUSINESS

Kingdom-centered business
in a self-centered world

ISBN: 978-1-941213-74-2

Cover design and layout: Violet Hershberger

Illustrations by Jerron Hess
Front cover photos: shutterstock.com

Printed in the USA

Third printing: December 2018

TGS001794

Published by:
TGS International
P.O. Box 355
Berlin, Ohio 44610 USA
Phone: 330-893-4828
Fax: 330-893-2305
www.tgsinternational.com

# It's Not Your BUSINESS

Kingdom-centered business
in a self-centered world

*Gary Miller*

# *Table of Contents*

# *Introduction*

The sun rose slowly over the South China Sea, and thus began another day of suffering. It was July 4, 1979. For five days, ninety-three Vietnamese refugees had drifted on a dilapidated fishing boat without food or water. With no motor, sail, or even an oar, the leaky boat was little more than a floating coffin. As the hot sun crept higher, some of the mothers began to consider the unthinkable—wrapping their babies in rags and slipping them overboard. It was just too painful to watch their children suffer.

When the communists had taken over Vietnam, businessmen and wealthy families were in sudden danger. Many chose to risk survival on the open sea rather than face the wrath of the Vietcong. This group had made it safely to Malaysia. But the Malaysian government, overrun by thousands of refugees, had told them to get back in their boats so they could be towed to an island refugee camp. However, there was no such island. After towing them some twenty hours out to sea, the boat pulling them cut the ropes and headed back to Malaysia. Believing it to be a short trip, the refugees hadn't brought food or water.

Three-year-old Vinh Chung was one of the refugees facing death that July morning. Four boats had been towed out to sea, and he had extended family in each one. As the seas became rough, the boats had drifted apart. The other three eventually floated back to land, but Vinh's was carried by currents and wind farther out to sea. Finally, on this sixth day of drifting, a passing American ship spotted their little boat, and they were plucked from the sea. Little Vinh and his family were taken to the United States.

They arrived with nothing but the clothes on their backs. A local church provided housing for six months, and Vinh's father found a job in a fiberglass factory and began supporting his family of ten on $90 a week. Eventually Vinh's father was able to get a job at Rheem Air Conditioning in Fort Smith, Arkansas, where he earned $9 per hour. For twenty-three years he worked there. Even though they built air conditioners, the building was not cooled, and the working conditions were difficult. In Vietnam, Vinh's father had been an executive and part owner in a prosperous corporation. Now he sweated in the factory while the office staff sat at nice desks in the air-conditioned environment he used to enjoy.

Vinh grew up watching his parents work from dawn to dusk so their children could have a future. But Vinh's parents expected their children to work hard too. Only on Sunday, when they attended a nearby Vietnamese church, were they excused from work. Vinh's parents also expected their children to make excellent grades at the public school. This wasn't easy since none of them knew English, but somehow they did it. Others looked on and wondered at their work ethic, their frugality, and their passion for education. Men at work would laugh and tell Vinh's father to enjoy life a little. Vinh's fellow students also viewed the family as strange. All they ever did was work and study. But Vinh's father saw something the others didn't. He saw America as a land of great opportunity. While others complained about their wages and never having enough money to pay their bills, Vinh's father wanted his children to thrive. Vinh eventually graduated from Harvard as a medical doctor and wrote a book telling his family's story.

### Land of Opportunity

Vinh's book, *Where the Wind Leads*,[1] brings the reader face to face with a graphic reality: those of us who live in the developed part of the world, especially North America, have been given tremendous opportunity. There are few places in the world where one can arrive with absolutely nothing and in one generation see all of his children able to support themselves and contribute to society. In America someone can start a small business, work hard, and flourish. This is why millions of would-be immigrants still press in from every side.

In 2002 Vinh returned to Vietnam for the first time and was shocked at the poverty. His relatives in the other boats had drifted back to their home country and still lived in shacks with no running water. Their walls were plastered with newspaper, and his cousins slept on the floor. Vinh describes his thoughts as he met with his relatives: "Visiting Vietnam was like walking into a parallel universe—the life that would have been mine if the current had been a bit stronger or if the wind had shifted direction."[2]

Vinh concludes his book by saying, "I worked long and hard to get where I am today, but the humbling truth is that all my hard work has been possible only because of a blessing I received that I did nothing to deserve."[3] Though his family came with nothing, the simple fact that they lived in America meant they were rich. Jesus said, "For unto whomsoever much is given, of him shall be much required,"[a] and as Vinh recognized the tremendous gift he had been given, he realized that much would be required of him.

## Tremendous Opportunity

America represents only about 5 percent of the world's population, yet it controls 40 percent of the wealth.[4] Never in the history of man has there been such disparity in the world or such opportunity in one country. In America, Vinh's family found a place where hard work could be converted into financial success. Those of us who grew up in this environment often fail to appreciate the blessing we have been given. If you have lived under a stable government or been blessed by steady employment, you have been given tremendous opportunity. Compared to global reality, you have been given much.

But this business-focused capitalistic environment has not always had a positive effect on the church. Our conservative churches discuss almost every imaginable topic and come to conclusions. But when we get to business and wealth, for some reason we fall strangely silent. We don't know what to do with business. On the one hand we need to

---

[a] Luke 12:48

make an income, but on the other many seem to be more passionate about their businesses than about the Kingdom of God.

I want to invite you to rethink with me our view of business and occupational life. How should we relate to the business world? Should we stay as far away from commerce and the business arena as possible? Or is it possible that God has more in mind for our businesses and occupations than we have understood? My prayer is that, as you read, God will reveal more of what He has in mind, and that He will provide a clearer vision of how you can use your occupation for the Kingdom. If you are an employee, may all those who come in contact with you walk away sensing they have come face to face with someone who is purposefully laboring "together with God."[b] And if you are a business owner, may you more deeply realize that it's not your business.

---

[b] 1 Corinthians 3:9

# PART ONE

## *Business: How Involved Should I Be?*

# *Business and the Kingdom of God* 1

"The secret to being successful in retail sales is to place the highest markup on smaller, unnoticed items, and the lowest markup on products where consumers compare pricing.

"For example," my business professor continued, "if you own a photography store, you want to keep your pricing as low as possible on your cameras. The average customer will call all over town to find the cheapest camera.

"But when that customer comes to your shop to purchase that low-priced camera," the instructor added with a crafty smile, "he will also purchase an extra lens or two, a tripod, and a nice leather camera case to protect his investment. And do you know how much thought he will have given to the markup on all these extra items? None."

Then, with a lower voice that trembled with excitement at the secret he was about to impart, he said, "It is on these little items, the very place the consumer is least suspecting, where you will make your profit!"

The professor in my business class went on to explain how a shop might mark up that expensive camera only a small amount, while the accessories might be marked up 400 to 500 percent.

"The unsuspecting customer has no idea what just

occurred. He will cheerfully go out and brag to his friends about the great deal he got, and more shoppers will visit your store!"

The lesson was obvious. The goal is to find subtle ways to extract as much as possible from the unsuspecting customer, while making him think he is getting the best deal in town.

### So That's How Business Works!

I remember leaving class that day with a new appreciation for the deceitful methods being used by successful retail businesses. We learned about loss leaders, the art of arranging products on shelves, and how to create longings and get customers to purchase more than they had intended. While there's nothing wrong with attractive displays or loss leaders, the motive of enticing customers to buy more seemed suspect. I finished that class with a nagging question. Would Jesus be a good businessman? Would the Man who said, "I am the truth," employ cunning schemes to fool His customers? And what about His followers? How involved should they be in this thing we call business?

Sometimes it seems our spiritual lives would be more vibrant if we didn't need to go out and work each day. We can visualize the Kingdom of God growing unhindered by occupational restraints. We would have plenty of time to help our neighbors whenever they have a need, and be able to involve ourselves in all kinds of "spiritual" activities, unhindered by the cares of this natural life. For many years believers have wrestled with thoughts like these, and some have concluded that following Jesus means putting as much distance as possible between themselves and money and business. In fact, some have concluded that believers should return to bartering and avoid using money to keep track of who "owns" what. Books have been written on the evils of the current monetary structure, and some speak of withdrawing from the banking system that the developed world employs.

In 1876 George MacDonald published a novel titled *Thomas Wingfold, Curate*, later reprinted as *The Curate's Awakening*.[1] The story circles around the life of a young Anglican minister, or curate, whose faith was challenged by a vocal atheist. As a result, this young curate reevaluated his life to see whether he actually believed what he was teaching.

As in most of MacDonald's books, there is a strong emphasis on living out the teachings of Jesus. The novel is written to challenge those in his day who were following the dogmas of men while ignoring the words of the Man they claimed to follow. Toward the end of the book, one character has a vision speculating how commerce might be conducted if men's hearts were pure.

This character, Mr. Polwarth, was taken by a heavenly guide to a dry goods store to observe how business was conducted. As he watched the interaction between customers and shopkeepers, he noticed something unusual. As each customer described his need, the friendly clerk quickly found the needed product. The customer took it, thanked the clerk, and headed back out onto the street. But no money changed hands. Indeed, the clerks didn't even write down the quantities being taken. Customers just came in, received what they needed, and departed.

Mr. Polwarth assumed the shopkeepers must have exceptional memories, but when he asked his guide to explain, he was told to just continue watching. The shop was crowded with many clerks and customers engaged in transactions, when suddenly one of the customers dropped to his knees. Instantly all the other people in the shop, customers and clerks alike, fell on their knees in prayer. After a few moments the customer who had first begun to pray rose to his feet, bowed to the others in the room, and with tears coursing down his cheeks left the store, and the establishment resumed business.

Mr. Polwarth watched all this in his vision and was confused. He asked his guide to explain what they had seen. Why was no money exchanged and nothing written down? And why did everyone in the store begin praying at once? Was it just the time for prayer in this town? The heavenly guide explained the lack of money by saying, "Where greed and ambition and self-love rule, there must be money; where there is neither greed nor ambition nor self-love, money is useless."

**Life Without Money?**

In this utopian economy of free exchange there was no need of keeping track. Each individual just shared what he was capable of contributing. No one needed to store up supplies. They took what they needed when they needed it and shared as others had need.

This was so different from the economy Mr. Polwarth was accustomed to. Of course he had many questions. "Suppose a man became greedy? What would happen if someone began to hoard or take more than he needed?"

The guide told him that was the cause of the collective prayer. The customer who first fell to his knees had been tempted by the thought of accumulation. He briefly entertained the idea of taking more than he actually needed and immediately fell on his knees in terror and shame. The others in the shop knew what had happened and instantly stopped their activities to lift up this fallen man in prayer.

Reading George MacDonald's fictitious description of utopian business, one has to wonder what such a world would be like. Is commerce as we know it something God can bless? How does God intend for us to apply Jesus' teachings in our occupations? And what about business ownership? Should believers be involved?

In preparation for this book, I designed a small survey and interviewed many people of differing ages and income brackets. I chose only people whom I viewed as serious about following Jesus. My goal was to find out how they viewed business and what place they believed it should have in a Christian's life. In my survey I asked the following questions:

1. If you hear that a Christian businessman has 100 employees, is your first thought positive or negative?

2. Rate the occupational options below from 1–4 according to how you view them. Do you assume a man is more spiritual if he:
   a. Is an employer?
   b. Is employed by someone else?
   c. Has a small family-based business and works at home?
   d. Is a missionary?

3. Do you believe God calls some men to be foreign missionaries?

4. Do you believe God calls some men to be businessmen?

5. Can a man who is trying to follow Jesus in everyday life

become the owner of a large business?

6.  Can an owner of a large business meet his other obliga-
    tions? Will it preoccupy him and keep him from being a
    good father?

It didn't take long to discover that business, size of business, and business ownership are controversial topics. Some see business as a wonderful thing, while others see it as something the follower of Jesus will avoid as much as possible. But I found that most believers fall into one of three basic categories.

## Production Paul

Production Paul owns a successful business and sees his work as simply being a good steward of the abilities God has given him. He is perfectly comfortable with commerce and being part of the business world. He likes efficiency, organization, and making things work. In fact, he can't understand why more men don't have their own businesses; he suspects it is a result of laziness. Production Paul enjoys the challenges that operating a business brings his way and sees the world of commerce as a source to fund relief for the poor and further the Kingdom of God. He also frequently speaks of the blessing of employment that Christian businesses provide. "Of course we need Christian businessmen," Production Paul likes to remind people. "It wouldn't be good if all of our men had to work in an ungodly environment."

## Larry Little

Larry Little has listened to all of Production Paul's arguments, but he isn't quite so sure. Larry acknowledges that there are godly businessmen whose abilities provide a financial blessing to the Kingdom. But he is concerned about men like Production Paul. Larry Little sees these businessmen start out with good intentions, yet over time become ensnared, either by debt when things don't go well, or by wealth when successful. Larry Little is afraid of big business. He likes and promotes home-based businesses, where children can learn to work alongside their parents. It isn't business that Larry Little is opposed to, but big business. He would like to see the church put some limits on how large a business may grow. One of Larry Little's friends recently heard him say, "When a business grows to where you have employees managing employees, that business is too big." Business, to Larry Little, can be a blessing when small, but very dangerous when large.

### Servant Sam

Servant Sam has listened to the discussion regarding business and has come to a different conclusion. He sees business ownership as dangerous and something to be avoided if at all possible. He has watched men start small businesses with good intentions, only to become successful, make lots of money, and eventually become ensnared by wealth. These men had no intention of building large businesses, but they were hard workers, found themselves in a good economy, and underestimated the power of riches. Servant Sam believes we are at times forced to become involved in the business world because we live on a cursed earth, but the less involvement the better. Because of his observations, Sam believes followers of Jesus should be servants—individuals who never aspire to business ownership or financial success by worldly standards. Servant Sam cannot comprehend how someone could end up owning a large business if he is sincerely trying to imitate the life of Jesus, a man who didn't even have a place to lay His head.[a] Big business, to Servant Sam, is incompatible with the character of Christ, and it is hard for him to fathom one of Christ's followers ending up in a corporate corner office. Servant Sam was recently overheard telling one of his friends, "Business as we know it is less than God's best, and we should avoid becoming ensnared by it." He likes to visualize a world like author George MacDonald's, in which each person shares of his abundance, receives from others when there is a lack, and no one bothers to keep track of who owns what.

### Conclusion

Production Pauls, Larry Littles, and Servant Sams sit side by side on our church pews each Sunday. They nod in agreement when the preacher speaks out sharply against love for the world and money. They shake

---

[a] Luke 9:59

their heads together at the foolishness of materialism. They agree that believers are called to provide materially for their own families, yet their views of business and how it relates to the Kingdom of God are entirely different. However, they don't need to worry that their differing viewpoints will be exposed. The topic of business ownership, size of business, or how involved in business a believer should be is rarely, if ever, discussed during a church service. All three are free to carry their own opinions without fear of conflict.

But each has strong opinions on business, and each has substantial evidence supporting those opinions. Their different gifts, personalities, and life experiences have helped create their worldviews. Consequently, they observe life and business from very different perspectives. In the next three chapters, we'll try to see business and spiritual life through the eyes of a Production Paul, a Larry Little, and a Servant Sam.

# "The Lord Will Provide" 2

The initial discussion had been lively, but now the crowd quieted and a new level of anticipation permeated the room. Several young mothers strained to see, and even the small children seemed to understand something exciting was afoot. Fathers shifted nervously in their folding chairs, wondering how their lives would be affected. Even the youth were more attentive than normal.

For several years the church had debated the need for a fellowship hall. Some thought the congregation was large enough that it should consider planting a new church in another area. Others disagreed. The church school was already struggling financially, they pointed out, and families moving away would make the situation even worse. So finally, after many meetings and much discussion, the church decided to add on a multipurpose room to the church building to accommodate their growth.

As the chairman of the building committee tacked the large blueprint to the wall, people began to grasp the magnitude of the proposal. A murmur of surprise

rippled across the room. The addition was obviously larger than most had expected. Hands began to go up, and questions were directed to the chairman.

"Do we really need something that large?"

"How much will this cost?"

"When we agreed to add on a fellowship hall, I was visualizing something about half this expensive," said a young father.

"Remember what happened when we built the church?" retorted another. "We thought we could never do it, but the funds seemed to come in as they were needed. An addition like this would really be nice."

"Lots of things would be nice," chimed in a third, "but I think we should consider something a little smaller."

Back and forth they went, and finally Robert[a] couldn't keep quiet any longer. "I think we are forgetting something," he said, looking around the group and pausing impressively. "Remember the question the Lord asked when Abraham didn't think it was possible for Sarah to have a son? The Lord asked Abraham, 'Is any thing too hard for the Lord?'[b] Abraham's faith was weak, and God wanted Abraham to trust Him to do the impossible. That is our problem tonight. We need to have more faith!

"We already heard what happened when we built the church. Some of you said the price was too high, but the Lord provided! As I look at this blueprint tonight, I think we are aiming too low. We should make the addition larger for future expansion. Let's think big and trust the Lord for the financial part. If we just have enough faith," said Robert as he took his seat, "the Lord will provide!"

## Who Will Provide?

Norman listened to Robert's passionate speech with mixed emotions. Norman owned a large furniture-manufacturing plant, and Robert was one of his many employees. Just that afternoon Robert had been in Norman's office asking about another loan, and throughout the years Norman had bailed him out of several financial difficulties. This time

---

[a] Names and details of stories have been changed throughout the book to protect identity.

[b] Genesis 18:14

Robert wanted to do something special for his anniversary and was a little short on cash.

Robert wasn't the only head of household sitting in that meeting who was short on cash. Looking over the group, Norman was keenly aware that he was the anonymous donor who had provided most of the funding for the last building project. Several individuals in this group currently owed him money, and he knew enough about their finances to know that little would be coming from them. Without his financial help, this building project would never happen. When they said, "The Lord will provide," he knew who they meant.

## A Difficult Start

Norman had been only three years old when his father died, and he grew up learning how to do without. They never would have survived without help from their local congregation, and Norman had many memories of people donating food, clothes, and secondhand appliances. Their family never knew what it was like to buy a new refrigerator, mattress, or piece of furniture. Their car was always an older vehicle donated by a brother in the congregation. While Norman appreciated all these gifts, he secretly resolved that someday things would be different. He knew it would be an uphill battle with no one to help him. But he didn't want to live the rest of his life receiving gifts from others.

Norman started working for an electrical contractor when he was just twelve years old. While the other boys played ball after school, he spent his afternoons sorting supplies and organizing the stockroom. He was a hard worker, and consequently his employer gave him a better paying job as soon as he finished school. Norman knew it would be difficult to get ahead on his hourly wages alone, so in the evenings after work he began making wood parts for a nearby furniture business. Late into the night he worked, producing as many components as he could and saving as much money as possible. It was hard to spend all his time in the garage working while his friends bought nice cars, new rifles, and the latest clothes. They called him a tightwad and made fun of his frugality. But Norman was determined to rise above the poverty he had experienced as a boy, and he didn't have the luxury of a father who was willing to provide financial assistance like some of the other boys had.

**A Risky Proposition**

Just ten years after completing school, the furniture factory Norman had been making parts for called him in for a meeting. They thanked him for the quality products he had been providing but informed him they would no longer need his services. They planned to dramatically increase production and had received pricing from another source. Not only could this competitor produce as many parts as they required, but by using computerized equipment, they could also do it for a substantially lower price. The bottom line was, they just couldn't afford to continue using him.

Norman was stunned. For the last couple of years he had been entertaining thoughts of leaving his electrical job and going into full-time furniture work. The environment at his job was less than desirable, and he had hoped to eventually be able to work at home. Now he was losing his only account.

"We really feel bad about it," his buyer told him, "but since you aren't able to produce the quantity we need for the price we can get it somewhere else, we really don't have any choice. Of course, if you had computerized equipment and could produce parts for the same price your competition is proposing, we would rather buy from you."

Norman asked for a few days to think things over. He checked out new equipment to see what his options were. The prices shocked him. Even if he used all his savings and got a loan, the payments would be high, and it would be a good many years before he could pay it off.

He shared his dilemma with several older men in his congregation. They were hesitant. "You might be able to pull it off," the first one told him, "but the risk is huge." The second brother agreed that there was a great deal of risk in the proposition. But knowing how much Norman wanted to escape the ungodly influences at work, he told him he would help obtain financing if Norman decided to proceed. After much prayer, Norman decided to quit his job, purchase the equipment, and produce furniture components full-time.

Those first few years were extremely difficult, and a couple of times

Norman wasn't sure his business was going to survive. He had quickly outgrown his mother's property, so it was back to the bank to purchase land and build a new shop. The market kept changing, new equipment was required, and more machinery meant more space. Several times he had to add on to his small factory. Production was growing, the number of employees was growing, and his debt was growing. Sometimes Norman felt like a man laying railroad track with the train engine right on his heels.

### The Reward of Diligence

Finally, after about fifteen years, Norman began to sense that maybe things were going to work out. Perhaps God had something more in mind than just his survival. Since the business had started, his primary goal had been to avoid defaulting on debt. But as the debt was repaid and profits increased, Norman found blessing in sharing. He knew what it was to be poor, and he found great pleasure in helping others. He had worked in an ungodly setting, and it thrilled him to walk through his factories and see young men working in a godly environment.

By this time Norman had about seventy-five employees, and he saw the potential to influence his employees' lives for good. He began providing seminars to teach his men to become good fathers and spiritual leaders in their communities. Some of his men came to him asking for financial assistance, and Norman found fulfillment in being able to help. He felt his diligence was finally paying off.

But all of this success also brought some things Norman never anticipated.

### The Secret Predicament of the Successful

Norman had tried to live a modest and frugal life, but regardless how hard he tried, he couldn't seem to avoid relationship problems. Many people came to him with financial needs, including his own brother, but he had found that loaning money was a path fraught with peril. If they failed to repay, there were few good options. To ignore the default proved that money was of no consequence to him. This widened the gulf between Norman and his brother who had borrowed. Reminding the brother of his unpaid debt just made him appear uncaring. After all, he was successful and didn't need the money. However he tried to help his brothers and sisters, it was rare for things to turn out right. Men in his congregation thought his business was too large, and even though many of them worked for him, they seemed to resent his success.

Tonight, as he sat through this building committee meeting, Norman felt he was again in an impossible situation. If he openly agreed with Robert and encouraged adding even more to the project, people would suspect he was just trying to demonstrate how little money meant to him. If he tried to encourage the group to go with a scaled-down version (which was really what he thought best), he would be viewed as stingy. So Norman kept silent.

But he couldn't shut off these mental ponderings. He was surrounded by brothers who had started out with many advantages he didn't have. While he had been working late at night in his mother's garage to start his business, young men like Robert had been playing sports and wasting money on cars and hobbies. It was hard for Norman to understand why they resented his success. Any of the men around him could have owned their own businesses. Some just didn't like hard work, and others were afraid of risk. Several had made poor financial choices. But any of them could have been as financially successful as he had been.

**The Hand of God**

Norman's business has blessed many people. It has provided funding for local needs, jobs for young men trying to get started, and assistance to missions in various parts of the world. As Norman looks back, he can see God's hand guiding him through all the mistakes as well as the successes. He doesn't believe everyone should have his own business and admits that God gives different gifts to His children. But he does believe God has called him to be a business owner. Even though some men in his congregation believe his business is too large, he believes he is doing what God has called him to do. Norman sees his business as a machine created by God to further His Kingdom. To dismantle it would be to walk away from where God has called him.

**Conclusion**

Norman enjoys industry and the challenges business brings. He views himself as a steward of the gifts and abilities God has placed in his care. He sees God actively involved in the business world and can't understand why fellow believers are so critical. While acknowledging that business ownership may not be for everyone, he would like to see more men work hard, take risks, and build their own businesses. In fact, Norman is currently mentoring a couple of young men, hoping to help them get started. Norman is a Production Paul. It is obvious to him that business is a blessing to the local church and the Kingdom of God—more than his brothers and sisters will ever realize.

But obviously not everyone agrees. We haven't all had the same life experience as Norman, and we don't all see the business world through the same lens as the Production Pauls among us. Larry Littles see ownership of business as acceptable, but only if growth is controlled and kept small. Let's look at another story that demonstrates why some have come to his conclusion.

# *Business Without Boundaries* 3

It was a beautiful fall afternoon as Bill and his friend Chris drove home from a relaxing day of fishing. Bill was a hard worker with great plans for the future, and a day off to fish was rare. As they bounced along in his old pickup, Bill passionately described his plans to build a large, successful business. Both Bill and Chris were recently married and faced the challenge of keeping food on the table and the bills paid. Yet Bill, much more than Chris, was determined to prosper financially. He didn't believe God wanted him to just subsist year after year, barely staying ahead of the bills.

"Do you really think," Bill asked, waving his arm expansively, "that God intends for us to just barely survive? He has given us good minds, the ability to work, and a thriving economy. Doesn't He expect us to make use of these gifts?"

Bill continued enthusiastically. "And how can we share with others if we are hardly making enough money to pay our bills? I think God wants us to produce plenty so we can bless others!"

Bill's father had been a hardworking man and had taught Bill diligence from a young age. Yet, although his father had labored industriously year after year, there was little to show for his efforts. It was obvious that Bill's father was a better worker than a manager.

Bill had observed all of this in his youth and had begun to despise his father. As he was forced to crawl out of bed each morning and head out to the field, hours before his friends, questions circled through his mind. *Why do we work so hard, yet have so little? Why do other people have nice homes, new cars, and long vacations without working as hard as my family?*

Bill concluded early in life that good management was the key to financial success. Now that he was married and starting out on his own, he couldn't wait to put his plans into action. With little fear of debt, great confidence in the economy, and a willingness to work, he could see nothing on the horizon to upset his plans. The fact that he was renting his house, had little money in the bank, and had almost no chance of being promoted at his current job seemed insignificant. His father had no ability to help him get started in business like other young men, but that too seemed a small hurdle. Bill was optimistic that good management and hard work could overcome any problem.

But Chris was not so sure. To him big business was a great snare to a man's spiritual life. Chris could think of men who had been successful in business, but he couldn't think of any he desired to emulate. He saw wealth and prosperity as a spiritual curse in the lives of these men. So in a friendly way Chris began to push back.

"But Bill, if there is no danger in pursuing big business, why are there so few examples of godly men with wealth in our churches? And why did Jesus warn so strongly against wealth? I think God would rather have us be faithful servants of others. After all, hasn't God chosen the poor of this world who are rich in faith?"

"Don't blame wealth and big business," Bill countered. "It's really a heart issue. People just forget to keep their focus on God. Look at all the wealthy men in the Bible who were godly: Abraham, Joseph, Job, David, and the list goes on! Wealth and business are not the real problem. It's that people start trusting in money rather than in God. We should do the best we can with what God has given us, understanding that everything is owned by God and should be used for His glory."

### Conflicting Advice

Not all of Bill's friends discouraged his vocational ambition. Some of the older businessmen in his congregation saw Bill as a rising star, a man with real potential, and they encouraged Bill to use his God-given abilities. Some even provided a little financial aid to get him started, and it wasn't long before Bill was able to put his business principles into practice. By borrowing a little from these older men and by leveraging the few assets he had, Bill started a small retail business. His banker recognized Bill's potential as well, and he made sure Bill had access to all the funds he needed for expansion.

From the start it was obvious that Bill was a natural businessman, and his enterprise was soon a well-known and formidable force in the local economy. Just twelve years after starting his business, Bill opened a second store in a neighboring city. He entered the market there in a much stronger position, armed with a strong balance sheet, a proven bank record, and business acumen gained from experience. Bankers competed to invest in his efforts. Bill was a proven winner.

Chris observed Bill's business accomplishments and financial achievements, and when there was a financial shortfall in their private school, Chris rejoiced that Bill's resources were available. When someone needed help with a medical bill, Chris knew Bill could be counted on to help.

But some other changes were not as encouraging. Although Bill still attended church services as usual, his focus was shifting. As a young-married man, he had enjoyed discussing the teachings of Jesus and how they applied to daily life. Now if he entered spiritual discussions, he commented on the timing of prophetic events or other theological topics that had little application in practical living. He seemed increasingly uncomfortable with Scriptural subjects that challenged his way of life. Chris observed all this and was concerned.

**Time and Money**

Bill was an excellent delegator. He was able to spot potential in employees and quickly move them into positions with more responsibility. Consequently, even though his business was still growing rapidly, Bill found himself with more free time and money to pursue relaxing diversions.

While at one time Bill rarely could find the time to fish, he now frequently looked forward to getting away from the business rat race. He enjoyed guided fishing trips to some of the world's premier fishing spots. These trips cost several thousand dollars a day, but it wasn't hard for

Bill to justify the cost. After all, many of his business associates spent much more on leisure activities. He consoled himself with the thought that he had worked hard, and it was only right that he should get away from work occasionally. Didn't Jesus and His disciples take some time off and rest? But as the years went by, his trips consumed more and more of his time. So Bill purchased a second home in a resort area. Now he could enjoy fishing and still be with his family in the evenings.

Even though Chris wasn't as close to Bill anymore, he became increasingly alarmed. He remembered those early discussions regarding the danger of wealth. He knew Bill had never intended to lose his spiritual vitality, yet it was happening before his eyes. If Bill had deviated from one of the church's rules or standards, the church leaders would have responded quickly. Yet they couldn't address something this serious and deadly. The teachings of Jesus and example of the early church left little doubt about God's view of extravagant living, yet the church seemed powerless to address this issue and wake up Bill to his spiritual condition.

Several times Chris tried to talk to Bill and gently challenge him about his direction, yet these discussions never seemed to attain the desired effect. Bill seemed suspicious that Chris's warnings might be driven more by envy than a genuine concern for his welfare. Consequently, Bill withdrew from Chris and became even less involved with his church. He spent more time traveling, and spare time at home was spent more with business associates and fishing buddies. In just fifteen years, Chris had watched Bill change from a vibrant follower of Jesus to a lukewarm church member.

**Business Without Boundaries**

To Chris the problem was simple. Business itself was not the problem. It was a business that grew too large. To Chris, Bill's life was a fulfillment of Jesus' warning in the parable of the sower. The seed which fell among thorns represents individuals who become distracted by earthly things. "The cares of this world, and the deceitfulness of riches, and the lusts of other things entering in, choke the word, and it becometh unfruitful."[a] Though it was written some two thousand years ago, Chris saw this verse as a succinct description of the progression of Bill's business life.

In the beginning stages, Bill was able to verbalize good goals and a clear spiritual vision. He really wanted his business to bless the Kingdom of God. But the very thing he thought was going to bless his family and church became a snare. Like an out-of-control thorn bush, it just kept growing until it choked Bill's spiritual life. To this day, Chris remembers the days when they had open communication and were able to pray together and talk of spiritual things. But those days are over.

Bill is still a part of, and has a great appreciation for, his conservative church fellowship. He abides by their brotherhood agreements, attends church (when he is home), and has nothing but good to say about the leadership. Although his pastors are concerned about the continued growth and focus on business, they aren't sure how to respond. Several times they've had to call on Bill for financial assistance, and he has always been willing to share. So, because he isn't disobeying any brotherhood agreements and has the resources to help in time of need, they have come to see Bill as a good church member who has a weakness for excessive lifestyle choices.

Chris disagrees. To him it is obvious that Bill is in the clutches of the enemy and that the spiritual vitality he once observed is gone. He sees a man who, enamored with commerce and blinded to the danger of business growth, gradually slid into the very trap he had been so confident he could avoid. Chris is still puzzled at the church's impotence in setting size limits for businesses. The Apostle Paul warned the early church many years ago, "They that will be rich fall into temptation and a snare."[b] To Chris this verse could be paraphrased to say, "Those who desire big business and fail to control its growth fall into temptation and a spiritual snare."

**Conclusion**

Chris understands the blessing that business can be to the body of Christ

---

[a] Mark 4:19

[b] 1 Timothy 6:9

and is glad his sons found employment in good environments during their formative years. But he is increasingly convinced that business growth should be limited. He dreams of a church setting where leaders understand the dangers of big business and have the courage to warn and in some way control its growth. To Chris, Bill's business life is a living example. From the beginning Bill wanted to build a large business, and this desire caused his downfall. Because of his observations, Chris has become a Larry Little.

But yet another group in the church believes men like Chris aren't taking business dangers seriously enough. Servant Sams see the business world as too risky for the believer, and ownership as too dangerous. They have seen many examples of men who became ensnared by wealth, though they never intended to own large businesses. They see business ownership as a slippery slope. Where Bill fully intended from the beginning to be financially successful, other men got pulled in due to their love of production and efficiency. But the resulting wealth pulled them down as well. Let's look at a story that proved to one man that the business world is just too dangerous for a follower of Jesus Christ.

# *The Slippery Slope*  4

Growing up on a dairy farm, there was always plenty of work. With five energetic boys on his hands, Tom's father was thankful for something to keep them busy. The four younger brothers entered into the daily routine with enthusiasm. They loved the work and enjoyed the milking. In fact, Tom's brothers couldn't think of anything they would rather do. But Tom was different. Even though he worked just as hard as his brothers, he was bored by the milking routine. He couldn't stand the smell of the animals, and he was sure nothing in the world could be as uninteresting as working on a dairy farm.

Until something broke down.

If Tom could have had his way, he would have forgotten the cows and worked on machinery every day. Mechanical breakdowns brought challenge, and he loved to identify the problem, develop a solution, and get the machinery back into operation. And Tom had a knack for improving machinery in the process. He seemed to have a natural ability, even as a small child, to point out flaws in equipment and develop a superior design. Consequently, Tom was called whenever equipment broke down. Those days became the bright spots in his farming experience. But since these repairs were needed only on occasion, Tom began to long for the day he could escape the family farm.

Tom's father observed this with dismay. He had loved cows all his life and couldn't imagine why someone would choose to dive into the greasy bowels of a tractor instead of working in the barn. But he was a wise enough father to understand that God gives varying gifts, so he began to look for an occupation that might better suit his mechanically inclined son. Just down the road from their farm was a flour mill, and one day the owner, an older man, mentioned to Tom's father that he was looking for a young mechanic to assist him. Tom listened to his father describe the job possibility that evening, and he was instantly excited.

## The Perfect Job

Tom was soon hired, and it didn't take long for the mill owner to see that his new employee was perfect for the job. Not only was he good at repairs, but within a couple of weeks he had suggested some changes to the machinery that greatly increased production. As Tom grew in his understanding of the business, the owner turned more and more responsibility over to him. Within just a few years Tom had a good enough grasp of the business that the owner could leave on extended vacations without concern. Just five years after hiring Tom, the owner asked if he would be interested in buying the business, and offered to finance the purchase.

Twenty-six-year-old Tom jumped at the opportunity. It was a large undertaking, but Tom had always thrived on overcoming obstacles. The combination of owning the business, searching for ways to increase production, and paying off debt created an environment in which he flourished. His business expanded, and in just a few years production had doubled, making his mill by far the largest in the area.

Tom had other important things on his plate as well. He had a growing family, and more than anything else, he wanted to be a godly husband and father. Even though his business was expanding rapidly, he tried to spend time each day with his children, teaching from the Bible and praying with them. He also willingly submitted to everything his church asked of him, attending every service and helping with needs in his congregation. He was a busy man, but he had always loved to work.

Twelve years after buying the mill, Tom discovered a new milling process. Other owners heard about his new process, and as soon as it was patented, Tom began producing and selling machinery to other mills. Now Tom had two sizable and extremely profitable businesses. He had never given much thought to expansion, and owning a large enterprise had never been his goal. He had simply enjoyed his work, continued to look for ways to improve what he was doing, and expanded into new areas as opportunities opened up. Both of these businesses continued to grow, and by the time Tom was fifty, he was one of the wealthiest men in the area.

**An Intriguing Diversion**

Tom rarely took a day off, but one year his employees gave him and his wife a gift certificate to a bed and breakfast. It was on this relaxing trip that Tom first gave much thought to antique cars. He saw a restored Model T, one of the first ones built, and was fascinated. He did some quick research, talked with the man who had restored it, and ended up buying it. He had no intention of ever buying another antique car, but after taking the car home, he began to notice restored vehicles. He subscribed to old car magazines, and it wasn't long till his face became familiar at antique car auctions. Tom started attending these auctions simply out of interest, but soon he began to buy. He was selective as he added to his collection, and some were very valuable.

Within a few years Tom needed a better place to store these vehicles. So he built a large shop. Word of Tom's collection got out, and people began to call and ask to come see his display. Local schools brought children to see his antique vehicle museum. Tom found it satisfying to see young and old alike enjoying his antique car collection.

**An Expanding Pursuit**

Then Tom began to notice antique gas pumps. It seemed natural to add a few restored pumps to his collection. It made his exhibit even more interesting, and older people who stopped by really enjoyed talking about the days when these pumps had been part of their lives. As Tom searched for rare gas pumps, he began to notice old fuel station signs. Adding them to the section in his building where he displayed the gas pumps made his growing museum even more attractive. Then there were car dealership signs and old Quaker State oil signs. It seemed there was no end to the fascinating items he could collect, and since he had plenty of money to buy them, his museum grew by leaps.

### An Exclusive Pursuit

In all of these purchases, Tom was discriminating. He didn't buy items simply because they were old. They had to be restored to nearly original condition and have historical value. Consequently, Tom's growing museum was increasingly noticed by professional collectors. In fact, he had one of the most complete collections of certain antiques in the nation. He found himself excited and captivated each time a new auction flyer arrived in the mail, and he would spend hours poring over the catalogs, deciding which items would make a nice addition to his collection. Tom's businesses continued to increase in profitability, so there was plenty of cash to work with. Auctioneers knew Tom wanted the best and were only too glad to call when a particularly valuable item was on the docket.

### From Empowering to Awkward

As people continued to enjoy his display, some of their comments began to make him uncomfortable. Some of his Christian friends were visibly shocked at the scope of his acquisitions, and Tom became a little embarrassed. His wife occasionally asked him if he really needed to buy more, and this bothered him as well. Several years went by, and as Tom continued to purchase antiques, there were some awkward moments. As visitors walked in the door, he watched the looks on their faces, wondering what they were really thinking.

Tom suspected some were envious and wished they could afford to do this. Others, he was sure, were sickened by the ostentatious display of wealth. After all, it was no secret that it took a tremendous amount of time and money to procure all of this. After experiencing one of these awkward moments, Tom would have some internal wrestling with his conscience. But then he would go through some mental gymnastics and rationalize his hobby. *After all, there is nothing morally wrong with what I'm doing. My church leaders haven't said anything, and there are certainly worse things I could be involved in. In fact, this is educational. And how can it be wasting money when these things increase in value? It's a good investment.*

## The Wakeup Call

A thought-provoking sermon on stewardship deeply challenged Tom. Something down inside didn't feel good, and for the first time he backed up and seriously examined the path he was on from God's perspective. The Holy Spirit worked in his life, and he gave serious thought to Biblical stewardship. If everything he owned was actually God's, were collections of antiques really what God was excited about? Something inside Tom began to shift. The massive display that just a couple of weeks ago had brought him such pleasure and fulfillment suddenly didn't. In fact, he began to feel repulsed by his excess. Just the sight of his collection nauseated him and brought an empty feeling. He knew something had to change, and after three weeks of misery, he called an auctioneer to say he wanted to sell as soon as possible. Overcome with remorse, Tom made an abrupt change in course.

## The Slippery Slope

When Tom first started buying antique cars, he was intrigued. He loved old machinery, and buying it seemed to connect him with past inventors and men who had a similar passion for mechanical engineering. He felt he was helping preserve history. But buying these cars soon became exciting. He connected with others who loved old cars, and he enjoyed the camaraderie. He found his passion to collect fulfilling. He knew few people were even able to afford these things. It made him feel special and successful. Without realizing it, he had gradually progressed from taking an interest in old cars to finding power, life, and personal exaltation from it.

"There is no question," Tom said soberly, "I was feeding on the power that buying brought me. I would go to auctions, and everyone there knew I would choose only the very best. Even the smell of those auction barns brought an adrenaline rush. I had a reputation, and I felt empowered even in the way auctioneers looked at me."

## The Constant Battle

Though Tom has changed course in life, the battle isn't over. Old habits are not crucified easily. Due to the residual income from his business, Tom still finds himself dealing with temptation. As we talked, he shared an example. Tom and his wife have never spent much on home decorating or furnishings. His wife has always been content, but recently Tom got to thinking it would be nice to upgrade their bedroom suite. So the two of them visited a furniture builder known for quality. They examined his work, discussed stain samples, and finally ordered a new quarter-sawn oak bedroom suite. It was an enjoyable day, and it wasn't till a few days later that he began to have some doubts. The price of over $6,000 hadn't seemed that excessive while in the cabinet shop observing the time and craftsmanship that went into the product. But lying in bed at night, Tom thought about what they were doing. As he imagined bringing the new furniture home, he found himself again becoming uneasy.

Was this really what God wanted them to do with this money? Was there really anything wrong with the old pine bed frame they had owned since first married? Tom and his wife discussed the situation and agreed they had made a mistake. They found it was too late to back out on the order, so they asked the furniture maker to deliver it to an auction where the proceeds were going to help people in need. Today, although Tom has a deep desire to devote the rest of his life to the Kingdom of God, he finds himself still tempted by the options wealth provides and isn't always sure what God wants him to do with his money.

But someone who lives close by views these constant dilemmas in Tom's life as completely unnecessary.

## A Simple Solution

Clyde lives just down the road and has for years worshiped in the same congregation as Tom. Clyde works in a local cabinet shop and has never had any interest in being self-employed or in taking risks. He likes the security of a weekly check, has always been able to pay the bills, and over the years has developed some strong opinions about how involved believers should be in the business world. He remembers when Tom first started working as an employee at the mill and when he became the sole proprietor. Clyde knows Tom well and knows his original goal was not to build a large business. Tom just kept walking through each door of opportunity that presented itself, and Clyde watched as the business became successful.

Clyde also watched with dismay as Tom began to collect cars. He became alarmed as the collection continued to expand. In fact, several times Clyde considered sharing his concerns with Tom. But due to fear of being misunderstood, he didn't go.

Clyde also watched in amazement as Tom made an abrupt change in course late in life. But in Clyde's mind big business, the hassle of maintaining possessions, and the ongoing temptations that excess money provides are totally unnecessary. As he watched Tom's journey from just down the road, the words and life of Jesus came alive in a new way. Clyde is willing to concede that there might be a place for self-employment to enable a man to work with his children, but in his mind a faithful follower of Jesus will simply be a servant of others. Any further involvement in business is a slippery slope and causes needless temptation in a believer's life. For a Servant Sam like Clyde, the simple solution is to avoid business involvement.

**Conclusion**

In the past several chapters we have looked at the lives of several businessmen and some deductions that have been drawn from their experiences. You have also had life experiences, and most likely you are drawn to one of these conclusions more than the others. Maybe you are a Production Paul, enjoying the challenge of business and wondering why others don't get more involved. Or perhaps you are a Larry Little and view the world of business as dangerous yet acceptable if things are kept in check. Or maybe you have seen so few good examples of Kingdom-focused business that you have decided the safest route is to withdraw as much as possible.

My goal in this book isn't to persuade you that one of these viewpoints is totally correct or completely wrong. Rather, it is to help you wrestle with some realities and find the path that God is calling you to. We need to understand that business and wealth can ensnare a man, yet we also need to grasp the potential for the Kingdom in our daily business interactions.

So far we have looked primarily at the difficulties and temptations that accompany business. But before you consider where God may be calling you, maybe we should take a closer look at the blessing of work and industry.

# *The Blessing of Industry* 5

Driving into the city of Managua, one cannot help but notice the young men lounging along the trash-littered Nicaraguan streets. They lean against doorways, sit on curbs, or find relief from the midday heat under an overpass, staring at you with bored expressions. The vehicle rounds a corner, and you are presented with yet another picture of able-bodied men listlessly waiting for opportunity. As you wind your way through the streets, the supply seems endless—masses of strong, intelligent, healthy young men doing nothing but watching traffic pass. And no wonder; a 2011 report stated that 40 percent of young Nicaraguans are unemployed, and 50 percent live in poverty.[1] These young people while away their time, some surviving by finding occasional jobs and others becoming involved in illegal activities such as drugs, theft, or prostitution.

Of course, Managua is not alone. It is but one of many cities, some much larger with conditions even worse, where people roam the streets, beg, scrounge

through dumpsters, and even live on top of city landfills in hope of finding something to feed their families for the day. Many of these people would love to be involved in any kind of business—anything productive that could provide a steady source of income. Those who do secure some type of employment are expected to share, not only with their own families, but with others as well.

Lack of industry and business in a society brings ills other than poverty. Youth grow up learning that stealing, selling illegal drugs, or begging from foreigners can be more profitable than honest labor. Time goes on, another generation comes along, and the problem compounds. When a society lacks productivity, you can expect to find violence, fear, material poverty, theft, and a basic lack of trust.

## We Forget

In the developed world we tend to forget this picture. We observe the materialistic rat race. We read of corporate takeovers, business owners who purposefully and repeatedly drive their companies into bankruptcy, and the great financial imbalance between business owners and their employees. In 2011, street demonstrations even broke out across America, with marching protesters calling for income equality. These rallies, known as Occupy Wall Street, were an attempt to expose the wealthy businessmen who were raking in millions of dollars with little regard for the plight of the common laborer. While the employees of these large corporations have trouble paying their rent each month, the owners use the corporate jet to travel between their several homes.

We listen to all of this and begin to perceive the average businessman as egotistical, selfish, and ruthless. We begin viewing business as having an inherent bent toward evil. Commerce becomes synonymous with the kingdom of this world. Surrounded by greed and self-centered business practices, it is hard for us to imagine the Kingdom of God being advanced through business. Satan is obviously using the business world to advance his agenda. Is it even possible that business could be used by God?

What does the Bible say about labor? I hear people speak of labor as though it is a result of the Fall. They seem to think Eden was a place where Adam just folded his hands behind his head, sat in his recliner, and enjoyed what God had created. But notice, Adam was given a job *before* he sinned. Work was not the punishment for sin. Labor is the customary activity of every normal and fulfilled man. When God created Adam and placed him in the garden, He gave Adam everything required to be perfectly content. Adam had healthy food to eat, pure water to drink, and a rewarding relationship with God. These have always been requirements for man's happiness. But there was one more thing Adam needed—a job.

### The Need to Be Occupied

God created man for labor. Not providing work for Adam would have been as foolish as creating fish to swim without providing water. The Bible says that God put Adam in the Garden of Eden "to dress it and to keep it."[a] When Adam fell into sin, his punishment wasn't that he suddenly needed to work and depend on the soil to produce his food. This was already the case. When Adam sinned, God said,

> God created man for labor. Not providing work for Adam would have been as foolish as creating fish to swim without providing water.

"Cursed is the ground for thy sake; in sorrow shalt thou eat of it all the days of thy life. Thorns also and thistles shall it bring forth to thee; and thou shalt eat the herb of the field."[b] Notice, the result of the Fall was not labor; it was working with cursed soil. Before the Fall, labor had always produced the desired results. Now things didn't always turn out as planned. For the first time thorns came up, insects devoured plants, and crops failed. The consequence of cursed soil was more labor and less production.

Sometimes in our affluent society we forget our great need to be physically occupied and the importance of work and industry. Americans

[a] Genesis 2:15

[b] Genesis 3:17, 18

have a strange culture. We do all we can to avoid physical labor and then go to a gym to exercise. I have seen people driving around in a YMCA parking lot trying to get a spot close to the door so they don't need to walk so far, only to go inside and exercise. What an amazing society! Where else on earth can you see people mowing their lawns with riding mowers and then going in the house to work out on the treadmill? Even as we do our best to avoid work, we understand that labor and exercise are important to our physical and mental health. Labor is important to us, and business is the environment in which it happens. But there is more! Before we overreact to the abuses and self-centered attitudes we see in the business world around us, let's look at a few blessings work brings into our lives.

## Occupational Blessings

Recently I was listening to a brother share some things that have impacted his Christian life. "One of the things that really influenced my teenage years was working for Joe," he said. "I know I wasn't always the best employee, but even when I wasn't diligent, he was always so patient with me, and he taught me many things." Later another man from the same community made similar comments about his time working for Joe and the blessing it had been in his life. It was obvious that Joe had been an effective mentor to youth in his community.

Joe was an older man who raised vegetables and sold them in the local markets. During the spring he hired many young people from his church to help with planting, weeding, and irrigating the crops. This provided a good place for youth to burn energy, earn some money, and perhaps learn some life lessons. Joe probably never knew the influence he had on these young people's lives. He was just trying to earn a living and bless those he encountered in the process. Business was the vehicle that provided this opportunity.

I have talked to many businessmen who spend considerable time assisting their employees with personal problems. Some have large businesses and are good delegators, which gives them time for counseling. Learning while working beside others has been a great blessing in my life. Those I worked with probably had little idea what influence their comments or responses in difficult situations had on my life. Christian businesses can provide many wonderful opportunities for mentoring.

**Opportunity to Bless**

The Apostle Paul told Timothy, "Charge them that are rich in this world, that they be not high minded, nor trust in uncertain riches, but in the living God, who giveth us richly all things to enjoy."[c] This is a familiar passage with a clear warning. But sometimes we focus only on the danger of industry and wealth and forget the potential blessing. The next verse says, "That they do good, that they be rich in good works, ready to distribute, willing to communicate."[d] This is quite a checklist.

Why did Paul want Timothy to tell the wealthy to do these things? It's because they are the ones capable of doing them. The man who is barely paying his bills isn't always able to distribute and share. He may be able to bless in other ways, but those who are rich in this world's goods will need to do most of the heavy lifting in this area. Most of us can probably think of godly businessmen who have shared with us out of their abundance.

Paul told the church at Galatia, "As we have therefore opportunity, let us do good unto all men, especially unto them who are of the household of faith."[e] Successful business owners, perhaps more than any other group of people in the church, have opportunity to bless materially. God has invested in them certain abilities, and He expects a return on His investment. The ability to give is one of the blessings of industry. At times we may focus too heavily on this one, but it is important that we recognize its importance.

**Demonstrating the Character of God**

On a summer day in 1948, George de Mestral, a Swiss mountaineer, took his dog for a walk. Returning after a long hike, George found that he and his dog were covered with little burrs. Intrigued, he took several burrs in the house and placed them under a microscope. Looking at the burrs under magnification, he noticed with interest the tiny hooks

---

[c] 1 Timothy 6:17
[d] 1 Timothy 6:18
[e] Galatians 6:10

that enabled the burr to cling so tenaciously to his pants.

*What if I could develop a two-sided fastener?* George thought. *One side with stiff hooks like the burrs, and the other with soft loops like my pants? Zippers are nice, but imagine how much faster this could be!* He instantly thought of many needs this would fill.

George's idea met with scorn and even laughter, but he was persistent. He found that nylon, when formed under hot, infrared light, forms tiny hooks for the burr side of the fastener. Together with a weaver from France, he perfected his new invention, and it was finally patented in 1955. Today, Velcro is a household word and a multi-million-dollar industry.[2]

> "Whether a man believes in God or not, when he restores, repairs, or produces, he is demonstrating a characteristic of God Himself."

We as men have a natural desire to improve and an inner craving to create. When we see a need, we enjoy developing a product or providing a service to solve the problem. Most businesses are simply putting this desire into action. This is another way business fulfills God's purpose. Whether a man believes in God or not, when he restores, repairs, or produces, he is demonstrating a characteristic of God Himself.

The Bible begins with a tremendous demonstration of God's ability to create. He miraculously formed the marvelous, orderly universe we see today from a cosmos that was without form and void. In both the physical and spiritual realms, God fixes problems and transforms chaos into orderliness. It is part of His nature. And these are also attributes of a good businessman. Whether he is a farmer transforming barren land into a productive field, a remodeler renovating a neglected house, or George de Mestral inventing Velcro, almost every businessman in some way demonstrates the image of the Creator. Many of these men may deny God's involvement and say He doesn't exist. Yet each time they develop new products, find better ways to do things, or make improvements to assist us, they portray the image of the One they deny.

## Conclusion

Throughout history, whenever God has designed something to bless mankind, Satan has come behind, attempting to twist it and transform it into something detrimental. Man's occupation and business have been no exception. Labor, one of the foundational components of the original creation, has become distorted. Today when we think of the business world, we do not usually equate it with godliness. Often our first thoughts go to greed, selfishness, and neglect of spiritual values. But this was not God's original intent.

Industry is a blessing, and followers of Jesus will be known for a good work ethic. Even Paul, speaking to the church at Ephesus, used his example of working hard physically to defend his ministry. He told them, "These hands have ministered to my necessities, and to them that were with me. I have shewed you all things, how that so labouring ye ought to support the weak, and to remember the words of the Lord Jesus, how he said, it is more blessed to give than to receive."[f] We don't usually talk about Paul's work ethic, but he wasn't ashamed of it. He provided, not just for himself, but also for others around him who had need.

[f] Acts 20:34, 35

# Trusting the "Christian" Businessman 6

In 1993 an exhausted, emaciated Greg Mortenson found himself wandering in the Himalayan Mountains. His goal to ascend to the peak of K2, the second highest mountain on earth, had failed, and he was now disoriented and lost, far from his climbing partners. As he stumbled through some of the most desolate reaches of Northern Pakistan, he happened upon an impoverished Pakistani village known as Korphe. Over the next seven weeks, this isolated Muslim community nursed Greg back to health. While recovering, he observed the village children. The poor village couldn't afford the dollar-a-day salary to hire a teacher, so would-be students sat outside scratching their school lessons in the dirt.

This determination to learn in the midst of abject poverty gripped his heart, and upon leaving he promised to return and build a school. He was grateful for the way these people had reached out to him, and he believed education could provide sustainable help. Upon returning home, Greg Mortenson immediately started a one-man campaign to help this remote Muslim village. He shared his experience with others to raise funds and made repeated trips back to one of the most inaccessible places on the globe. Over the next few years, Greg helped construct over fifty schools. As word of his endeavors got out, more funds became available, and he would return to build another school. This humanitarian effort eventually grew into a large organization known as the Central Asia Institute.

Immediately following the 9/11 terrorist attacks, the fascination with anything Muslim led to growing interest in Greg's work. Just who were these extremists who believed in something so strongly that they would fly a jet into a skyscraper? Some donors were intrigued with the idea of responding to the Muslim problem with schools instead of bombs, and consequently the work Greg was doing in Pakistan and Afghanistan attracted an even larger donor base.

In March 2006, Greg published a book titled *Three Cups of Tea*.[1] In gripping detail he described the challenges of working among radical Muslims. He told of being kidnapped by the Taliban, going toe to toe with enraged mullahs, and the fascinating details of the many death threats he had received. He also described the emotions he went through while being held by the Taliban and awaiting his execution, fearing that his pregnant wife back in the States would never know what had happened to him.

*Three Cups of Tea* was an instant success. People loved the thought of changing the world one school at a time, bravely going into the heart of Taliban country to make the world a safer place. Greg Mortenson became a hero. Money poured into Greg's Central Asia Institute, and by the spring of 2011, *Three Cups of Tea* had been a *New York Times* bestseller for four years. Greg Mortenson was an international celebrity, and for three consecutive years was on the short list for the Nobel Peace Prize.[2] Everyone seemed to believe that what he had to offer was exactly what was needed. Even President Obama donated $100,000 of his personal money to help with this work.[3]

**A Different Story**

Then on April 17, 2011, CBS aired a story on *60 Minutes* that cast Greg in a different light. They revealed that much of the book *Three Cups of Tea* was a fabrication. Instead of using the donated funds to build schools and educate Pakistani students, Greg Mortenson had been flying around the country in a Learjet and promoting his book. Millions of dollars were unaccounted for, and one of Greg's fans and a heavy supporter of his work ended up lashing out in frustration and writing a book called *Three Cups of Deceit*.[4] When the truth started to come out, Greg's co-author of *Three Cups of Tea,* David Oliver Relin, who had a passion for humanitarian aid, received heavy criticism for his involvement and journalistic work in the book. He became depressed, finally taking his own life on November 15, 2012, at age 49.[5]

Since then there has been much debate over the truth of all the allegations. Greg Mortenson confessed that some of the details in his book were incorrect and that accounting wasn't his strong point, yet he maintained he really was trying to help. Others have alleged that, while he has done some good, Greg's primary focus was self-centered— that even the good he did was with the intent of impressing others, and that he wasted valuable resources and embellished his own role.

We may never know who is correct in the ongoing debate over the accuracy of Greg's story or how effectively donations to Central Asia Institute were used. Regardless of how strong the defense, there will always be a certain suspicion surrounding this organization. It will be difficult for the average donor to keep writing out $25 sponsorship checks each month while carrying a mental image of Greg Mortenson flying to his next meeting in a Learjet. Once a non-profit has lost the confidence of its donors, trust is almost impossible to regain. Greg continues to give public presentations. He shows pictures, tells about the great need for schools, and explains how your donation could be a blessing in these Muslim communities. There is no question, the need is great. But it is hard to escape the past, and Central Asia Institute has had financial difficulty for an obvious reason. The public still struggles to trust Greg Mortenson. Yes, he was doing some good with the millions that poured in, but much was wasted on selfish pursuits and a self-centered lifestyle. He wasn't completely transparent and honest.

### A Lack of Trust

Christian businessmen often sense a similar lack of trust. Though they provide funds in their communities and churches, others view them with suspicion. In many cases the root cause of mistrust is the same. These owners profess that their businesses and all their possessions belong to God, yet in far too many cases they live extravagant lifestyles. People can only conclude that they aren't being completely transparent and honest. Like Greg Mortenson, these businessmen can point to great need. They may say funds are needed to further the Kingdom and point out the fact that their profits are being used to bless others. But it is hard to hear what they say when we see them living an affluent lifestyle.

When preparing for this book, I tried to locate and interview Christian business owners who were known in their communities for having a Kingdom-focused vision. I went to areas with large concentrations of conservative believers and looked for men who were operating big businesses with the primary goal of blessing the Kingdom. When I met with these owners, I asked many questions. All of them said they wanted their businesses to bless their local communities as well as the larger Kingdom of God. But one question was uncomfortable for some. I asked for the amount they paid themselves each year compared to the annual income of their top managers. If they truly desired to use resources for the Kingdom, this shouldn't have been a difficult question to answer, and thankfully for some it wasn't. In fact, some were taking less from the business than some of their top employees were receiving.

But to be honest, these men were in the minority, and I was only interviewing men with a reputation for being Kingdom-focused. There are reasons businessmen live under a cloud of suspicion. One person I interviewed told me, "There is a sense of entitlement in our business owners. They expand their businesses and then believe they can take the yearly Florida trip, buy the vacation home, and continually upgrade their homes." An owner of a large firm lamented, "The way we have used our wealth has brought reproach upon us." He was simply acknowledging that there is a shortage of men with the God-given gift of business who are able to handle the financial success it brings. Too

> One person I interviewed told me, "There is a sense of entitlement in our business owners. They expand their businesses and then believe they can take the yearly Florida trip, buy the vacation home, and continually upgrade their homes."

many use their resources in self-serving ways. Consequently, we have trouble trusting Christian businessmen.

## Businessmen: Potential Blessing to the Body of Christ

The Christian businessman has natural attributes and gifts that can be useful to the body of Christ. The church needs men with good leadership qualities and clear vision who can properly identify a problem, develop a solution, and put it into action. A good businessman usually possesses these abilities.

We need jobs to provide for our families, and it is a great blessing when men can work in a Christian environment. A Christian businessman can provide this. Money is needed to meet many of the needs in our world, both spiritual and physical. While many of us have difficulty getting all our bills paid, the successful businessman often has an abundance of discretionary income. We may want to share more Bibles with those who don't have them and provide more food for the hungry; we may know that widows and orphans are still being neglected, but often we lack the funding to fulfill the need. The businessman with his extra funds should be the perfect solution. So why don't we encourage more young men to become successful businessmen?

Take, for example, the need for Bibles in restricted countries. We would love to provide Bibles to all the believers in Asia who long for one. Yet due to the speed at which the churches have expanded, organizations are not even close to providing enough Bibles to reach this goal. Why not train our men to be successful in business so they can produce the needed revenue?

The answer is simple. We have difficulty trusting the "Production Pauls" among us. We listen to their expressed desire to expand their businesses so they can bless the Kingdom of God. We even go to them when our church or organization needs funds. But we question their motives and wonder how they use their excess funds. How many large business owners do you know who live in simple housing, drive inexpensive vehicles, and avoid any public demonstration of their financial success? Thankfully there are some. But somehow these are not the ones who generally come to mind when we think of wealthy Christian businessmen.

## Common Denominators

We have looked at the differences between how Production Pauls, Larry Littles, and Servant Sams view the business world. They go about day after day observing situations that support their points of view. There is some truth in the way each group views business. And as diverse and opposite as these three viewpoints may be, there are some common denominators. Let's look at a few Biblical truths on which they can all agree:

- **Business and wealth can become a spiritual snare in a believer's life.** Jesus said, "It is easier for a camel to go through a needle's eye, than for a rich man to enter into the kingdom of God."[a] There is great danger in too much emphasis on business, and it is possible for "the care of this world and the deceitfulness of riches"[b] to choke our spiritual lives. Industry may be essential to surviving in this world, but we are going to need to keep an eye on it.

- **A Christian work environment is a blessing.** Even those who believe we should avoid business as much as possible agree that it is a blessing to have a Christian employer. Ironically, many of the Servant Sams who are highly suspicious of Production Pauls are extremely thankful they work for one. Some have worked in ungodly environments and are not interested in going back. They can share multiple reasons why it is a blessing to work for Christian bosses.

- **Success should not be measured by a man's business achievements**. Everyone I interviewed agreed on this one. Jesus said, "A man's life consisteth not in the abundance of the things which he possesseth."[c] We know this is true, and we really want to believe it, so it isn't hard to agree verbally. Yet Production Pauls who enjoy business and view business ownership as good stewardship struggle to internalize

[a] Luke 18:25
[b] Matthew 13:22
[c] Luke 12:15

this one. Several confessed that money tends to become their scorecard for success in business. On the other hand, Servant Sams and Larry Littles have trouble with this as well. If we are suspicious of businessmen, it is easy to use size of business or wealth to judge. The larger the business, the more suspicious we tend to become of its owner, and the smaller the business, the more holy or virtuous we may consider him.

- **There are differing gifts within the body.** Even those who believe everyone should just be a servant conceded that God has given some men the ability of administration. Though these Servant Sams have no interest in business and carry a strong distrust for businessmen, they understand that if business is going to take place, someone will need to do it. Diversity of gifts within the church is a basic Biblical principle, and though our views and fears may be different, this is a truth we can all agree on.

But what about our differences? What about the successful businessman who professes to be following Jesus? Or the energetic young man who says he is expanding his thriving business for use in the Kingdom? Should we bless him in this pursuit? Can we trust him?

### Conclusion

Greg Mortenson has a problem. He really would like to persuade potential donors to contribute more to the Central Asia Institute. He says he has learned from his past and is trying to provide real, sustainable help to the many uneducated children in Pakistan and Afghanistan. I think that really is his desire. But his listeners still carry a mental image of him flying around in a corporate jet and living the high life. If he is going to restore confidence, Greg will need to live simply and frugally for a long time to restore the trust he lost.

Christian businessmen are in a similar position. They would like for business to be regarded as a legitimate pursuit and themselves as an integral part of the Kingdom of God. Yet until more financially successful businessmen prove that they can live simple lives and focus their resources on the Kingdom, many will have trouble believing the truth of their statements. There is a great need for godly examples—business owners who verbally acknowledge and demonstrate by their lifestyle choices that everything under their control is really God's.

# PART TWO

*Reconciling Jesus
and Proverbs*

# Getting What We Want from Scripture  7

Joel Osteen, pastor of the large Lakewood Church in Houston, reportedly lives in a $10 million house and has a net worth of over $40 million. His wealth, largely due to book sales, continues to rise. Joel views this as the blessing of God on his ministry. Joel is famous for teaching that God wants you to be wealthy, and his first book, *Your Best Life Now*, remained on the *New York Times* bestseller list for almost four years, selling more than four million copies.[1] Obviously his message of health and wealth resonates with the general public. Osteen teaches that God rewards the man who is faithful to Him with physical health and financial prosperity.

Is Joel Osteen's teaching Biblical? It is if you believe God is still working within the paradigm outlined in Deuteronomy. God's message was clear to those living in that time: Follow God and you will miraculously be blessed with health and wealth. You will get more rain, your crops will do better, and your animals will produce more. There are definitely Old Testament passages that support the health and wealth teaching.[a] There was a time when God's most obvious blessing was material prosperity.

But if you focus on the teachings of Jesus, you will arrive at a very different conclusion. Jesus never encouraged the accumulation of earthly wealth. While the message of Joel Osteen is popular and sells well, the message of Jesus never has.

---

[a] Deuteronomy 7:12–14, 28:1–14

## Finding What We Want

Most of us have talked with people who interpret the Scriptures illogically. They have a point they want to prove, so they find a verse that seems to say what they want and then use it to substantiate their point of view. Sometimes the verse is completely out of context and the contrived meaning has no connection to the original message. But none of this seems to matter. The most important fact at the moment is that they found a verse that says what they want. When our goal is to prove our denomination more doctrinally correct than someone else's, we can become particularly adept at this skill. This is a great abuse of God's Word.

History is replete with examples of misapplying Scripture. In the days leading up to the Civil War, professing Christians on both sides of the dispute used Scripture to validate their positions. Some risked their lives to hide slaves and help operate the Underground Railroad. They were trying to obey Jesus' command, "As ye would that men should do to you, do ye also to them likewise."[b] It seemed obvious that since they wouldn't want to be slaves themselves, they should do all they could to help people who were.

But the slaveholders used Scripture to justify their position as well. United States Senator James Henry Hammond explained his "Scriptural" position on slavery like this: "The doom of Ham has been branded on the form and features of his African descendants. The hand of fate has united his color and destiny. Man cannot separate what God hath joined."[2] Both sides were sure they were right, and both had found Scriptures to substantiate their claims.

Jefferson Davis, president of the ill-fated Confederate States of America, also confidently declared, "[Slavery] was established by decree of Almighty God. . . . It is sanctioned in the Bible, in both Testaments, from Genesis to Revelation. . . . It has existed in all ages, has been found among the people of the highest civilization, and in nations of the highest proficiency in the arts."[3]

It is amazing that men professing to adhere to the same Bible could

---

[b] Luke 6:31

come out so far apart. Even extremely vile men like Adolph Hitler have used the Bible to justify their despicable deeds. In many of his speeches, Hitler used Scripture to vindicate his position, even using events from Jesus' life to demonstrate why it was perfectly right to hate and persecute the Jews.

> In boundless love as a Christian and as a man, I read through the passage which tells us how the Lord at last rose in His might and seized the scourge to drive out of the Temple the brood of vipers and adders. How terrific was His fight for the world against the Jewish poison. Today, after two thousand years, with deepest emotion I recognize more profoundly than ever before the fact that it was for this that He had to shed His blood upon the Cross.[4]

It is hard to even imagine someone taking the life and teachings of Jesus, the one who came to save His chosen people, and twisting them to this extent. But let's not pass off these historical misapplications as though the days of abusing Scripture are over. These men wanted something, and they went to the Bible to find a verse that agreed with what they wanted.

Jefferson Davis believed in slavery. The economy of the South thrived largely because of slave labor. If all the slaves were suddenly emancipated, a tremendous amount of wealth would walk away, and owners would be left with no way to operate their plantations. Therefore, in Jefferson Davis's mind, slavery must continue, and he went to the Bible to find substantiation. Hitler hated the Jews, and annihilating them was a burning obsession in his life. When he read the Bible, it wasn't to find truth. It was to find justification for what he already desired.

As I read quotes from men like Hitler and Davis and observe the irrational ways in which they abused the Word of God, I have to assume you can find a verse to validate almost any doctrine, regardless how absurd. American Christianity can excuse almost any sin and find Scripture to justify it. You can find "Christians" who believe divorce and remarriage, going to war, and homosexuality are acceptable, and they use the Bible to confirm it.

So what are we to do? Is Scripture so vague that it allows for multiple interpretations? If the Bible can be used to justify the very thing it condemns, what good is it? The answer is both simple and sobering. The Bible has the potential to provide

> **The real question is not whether there is a Bible verse that agrees with what you desire. The more important question is, What do you really desire when you read the Bible?**

whatever you truly desire. If a man is seeking truth when he reads, then truth is what he will find. If he is seeking justification for his path, then justification is what he will find. The real question is not whether there is a Bible verse that agrees with what you desire. The more important question is, What do you really desire when you read the Bible?

## What Do You Really Desire?

As I look back over my life and see the gap between my lofty goals and actual daily choices, I realize I am not always a good judge of my own heart. Proverbs says, "Every way of a man is right in his own eyes,"[c] and I am fully capable of justifying positions in my life that are less than the best. As we look at controversial topics like Christian business, it is essential that we understand this. If our hearts secretly desire to accumulate wealth, we will have a tendency to focus on certain verses while ignoring others.

We seem to have an amazing capacity for justification. For example, we hear Production Pauls say we need to develop large businesses so that the profits can be used to bless others. But as we observe their lifestyles, this isn't what we see. Even though the stated goals sound spiritual, their carnal and affluent way of life proclaims that there are other secret longings in the heart.

But there is another side to this coin. I have observed Servant Sams, in reaction to the excesses of Production Pauls, focusing on certain verses while minimizing others as well. The desire to expose the "real"

---

[c] Proverbs 21:2

motives of the businessman can cause them to concentrate on verses that speak of the blessing of poverty, the danger of entanglement, and the warnings of Jesus to the rich, while skipping over verses that point out the need for diligence in material things. I have met Servant Sams who have neglected hard work for "spiritual" reasons. Our desires and longings have a huge impact on how we read the Word of God. This is why Jesus warned us by saying, "Take heed how ye hear."[d]

Inner longings also influence our interest in investigating context. When I find a verse that agrees with my personal views or longings, I generally have little interest in investigating the context in which the verse was written. And this does not just apply to reading Scripture. If I have a low estimation of a brother and then hear some negative news about him, I am not inclined to investigate the truth of what I have heard. But if I deeply admire someone and hear a disparaging comment concerning him, I will demand substantiation before accepting it.

As you search the Bible for God's will regarding involvement in business, you can find verses that seem to contradict others. For example, Jesus said a wise man will give thought and do some planning before he starts to build a tower.[e] That is only prudent. But He also said, "Take no thought for your life, what ye shall eat, or what ye shall drink."[f] Both of these verses are quoted by Christian business teachers to substantiate entirely different viewpoints. Often after I teach a financial seminar, people come up with questions regarding some statement I made, and almost always these people fall into one of two groups.

**"Focus on Proverbs" Group**

"The younger generation needs to go back and read what Proverbs has to say about diligence, saving money, and planning ahead. They need to learn from the ant! They don't want to start businesses and save for the future, and then when they get into trouble, they come running to us older ones for financial help."

Statements like these are common and typically come from the

---

[d] Luke 8:18

[e] Luke 14:28–32

[f] Matthew 6:25

Production Pauls, and sometimes even Larry Littles, among us. I also hear this from older men who have experienced hard times in the past. They have worked hard and created successful businesses and now are asked by their church to mentor the younger generation. They become frustrated with the younger men, who appear lazy, uninterested in providing for their own futures, and ignorant of some basic common-sense teaching that Proverbs has to offer.

### "Focus on the Teachings of Jesus" Group

"I don't understand the older people in my congregation. They seem consumed by business, getting ahead, and saving for retirement. Jesus told us clearly that we should sell what we have and give to the poor. He taught that the poor are blessed and that we shouldn't accumulate wealth. Yet some of the older members in our congregation are the wealthiest in our community. Jesus' words are not hard to understand. Why can't they just submit to what He said? We need more teaching on this."

Comments like these are also common in our communities, and they usually come either from Servant Sams or from younger men who are serious about following Jesus and have lost confidence in the older generation. They have watched some of the older men use profits from their large businesses or farms to indulge in a self-focused lifestyle, and they see these older wealthy men as ignoring some basic teachings of Jesus.

Two opposing viewpoints, and both use Scripture to substantiate their views. Depending on your age and experience, you probably identify more with one of these concerns than the other.

As I indicated earlier, we need to understand the power of our inner desires and be willing to honestly ask ourselves, "What do I really want?"

We also need to think about how we delineate Scripture. Does every verse, whether in the Old or New Testament, carry the same weight? Does context matter? Should the fact that a letter was written to a specific church with a particular problem be taken into account? I believe all Scripture is inspired by God, but I do not believe in a "flat Bible."

### A Flat Bible?

In other words, I don't believe every verse in the Bible carries equal weight. If we are going to work through seeming discrepancies in the Scriptures, it is important to take time to understand the context in which they were written. Several verses in the Old Testament, for example, teach that stoning is the proper punishment for some sins, while verses in the New Testament command us to love everyone, even our enemies. These are radically different teachings, and if we treated these verses equally, there would be endless debate. But Old and New Testament verses do not carry equal weight in our day. As we consider different passages of Scripture regarding business, we need to keep this in mind.

## Conclusion

Years ago I was working on a construction project when the owner told several of us to come outside. He had hired a water witcher to find water on his property, and he wanted us to observe. I had heard about dousing for water but had never observed it, so I watched as the man talked to the broken-off branches in his hand, asking them where the water was, how many feet it was down to the water, and how much water a well at this location would produce. Chills ran down my spine as I saw the small sticks bend as though pressed by an unseen hand in response to his questions. After he had finished, a couple of us challenged his involvement with water witching. We told him he was interacting with the forces of darkness, but he disagreed. He said he was a Christian and God had given him this gift.

"The Bible is very clear," he told us with confidence, "that the 'manifestation of the Spirit is given to every man to profit withal.' "[g]

While he didn't convince me that God had

---

[g] 1 Corinthians 12:7

given him this gift, I was persuaded of something else. You can find whatever you want in the Bible. In these next few chapters, we want to look at some of the tension that exists in Scripture regarding business and wealth. But it is essential that we are really looking for truth as we do this, for we will find whatever we are looking for!

# *Business and Proverbs* | 8

Turn to almost any American "Christian" financial counselor's writings, and you will find a focus on the book of Proverbs. Take Dave Ramsey, for instance. While he would say money isn't the most important thing in the world, his teachings are unashamedly intended to help you accumulate it. Dave Ramsey grew up in Tennessee, and early in life he had an interest in financial management and wealth. By his mid-twenties he was a millionaire, enjoying a successful career in real estate. Dave describes his early financial life like this:

> Starting from nothing, by the time I was 26 I had a net worth of a little over a million dollars. I was making $250,000 a year—that's more than $20,000 a month net taxable income. I was really having fun.[1]

But he was also heavily in debt and oblivious to the potential consequences. As a result, when the local economy went south, he lost everything. This experience had a tremendous impact on how Dave viewed business and debt, and he began to read the Bible and other material relating to finances. He also attended seminars and learned from Christian writers like Larry Burkett and Ron Blue. Soon Dave developed his own set of teaching materials based on his experience and what he had learned from others.

Today Dave Ramsey is a household name in America. His books can be found in most major bookstores, his materials are used in churches across the nation, and his voice is familiar on hundreds of radio stations. Using Scripture, he teaches people how to get out of debt, how to budget, and how to slowly accumulate wealth. It is a popular message, employing present frugality to enjoy future prosperity. "If you will live like no one else, later you can live like no one else," is Ramsey's familiar mantra, and millions of people are following his teachings.

But are Dave Ramsey's teachings correct? Are they really Biblical? His teachings have helped many recover from heavy debt loads, yet something about his message is different than that of the Jesus he claims to follow. I want to suggest that Dave Ramsey's teachings are built directly on the message of Proverbs.

**What Is the Message of Proverbs?**
When considering business, industry, and wealth, the book of Proverbs has several clear teachings. So, for a moment, set aside any preconceived ideas you may have about the problems regarding business and wealth in the church today and consider what the book of Proverbs teaches.

- **Common sense.** Proverbs abounds with statements of what we refer to as common sense. If you first do this and then that, the result will be this. "The sluggard will not plow by reason of the cold; therefore shall he beg in harvest, and have nothing."[a] This is simply a true statement of common sense. If you choose to stay in the warm house when you should be working in the field, you won't have a harvest. The book of Proverbs is awash with these kinds of profound statements. It is a collection of natural, observable truths about life and a book of common sense.

- **Self-preservation.** Throughout the book of Proverbs the reader is taught to be diligent lest he be taken advantage of or lose what he has. Notice the underlying message of these two verses: "Be not thou one of them that strike hands or of them that are surety for debts. If thou hast nothing to pay, why should he take away thy bed from under thee?"[b] These verses apply to what is called co-signing for a loan,

---

[a] Proverbs 20:4
[b] Proverbs 22:26–27

when one person pledges to share the risk with someone else. But notice the message. "Why would you do that? Why take that kind of risk? If the fellow you are co-signing the note for goes belly up, you might lose your own bed!" This same underlying thought pervades Proverbs. In essence, it teaches that there are consequences to choices we make in life. Don't make choices that might cause you to perish, to fall into mischief, or to be led into poverty. If you want to be successful, there are some things you should do and others you shouldn't.

- **Prosperity is the reward of diligence and frugality.** "He that tilleth his land shall have plenty of bread: but he that followeth after vain persons shall have poverty enough."[c] This message is interwoven throughout the book. If you work hard and are diligent, you will be prosperous. Proverbs also warns against seeking wealth by other means. "Wealth gotten by vanity shall be diminished: but he that gathereth by labour shall increase."[d] The path to prosperity is taught clearly in Proverbs. "He that loveth pleasure shall be a poor man: he that loveth wine and oil shall not be rich."[e] This verse says that the man who chooses to spend money on pleasure, living it up as he goes, will never accumulate much wealth. The path to wealth is hard work and a frugal lifestyle. It was true when Proverbs was written, and it is still true today.

- **Poverty is the reward of slothfulness.** The writer of Proverbs describes some things he observed while taking a walk. "I went by the field of the slothful, and by the vineyard of the man void of understanding; and, lo, it was all grown over with thorns, and nettles had covered the face thereof, and the stone wall thereof was broken down. Then I saw, and

---

[c] Proverbs 28:19

[d] Proverbs 13:11 (also see Proverbs 20:21 regarding receiving an inheritance)

[e] Proverbs 21:17

considered it well: I looked upon it, and received instruction. Yet a little sleep, a little slumber, a little folding of the hands to sleep: So shall thy poverty come as one that travelleth; and thy want as an armed man."[f]

This is another recurring theme in the book of Proverbs. Material poverty is the result of poor choices, laziness, and slothfulness. If you are going to extract food and blessing out of this cursed earth, you will have to work to do it. It will not come easily. Just as diligence and frugality have a reward, so does laziness. And the reward for slothfulness is poverty.

- **Planning and saving for the future.** In Proverbs the lowly ant is held up as an example. "Go to the ant, thou sluggard; consider her ways, and be wise: which having no guide, overseer, or ruler, provideth her meat in the summer, and gathereth her food in the harvest."[g] Notice, the ant isn't only a diligent worker, but it also plans ahead. God has placed within the ant the knowledge that summer doesn't last forever. So while there is plenty, the ant gathers and saves for the coming winter. The lesson here is evident. A wise man knows that if he is going to succeed materially, he will need to plan ahead and save during times of plenty.

- **Material wealth is a blessing from God.** Proverbs also shares some of the blessings of being rich. "The poor is hated even of his own neighbour: but the rich hath many friends."[h] This verse along with others says that a man who is wealthy will have more friends. Material wealth also provides some

[f] Proverbs 24:30–34

[g] Proverbs 6:6–8

[h] Proverbs 14:20; 19:4

earthly security. "The rich man's wealth is his strong city: the destruction of the poor is their poverty."[i] The rich man is able to defend himself against many things in life, another advantage to having wealth.

Different characters in the Old Testament, whom we hold up today as righteous men, were very wealthy. I believe this is a fulfillment of God's promise. One verse in Proverbs says it like this: "The crown of the wise is their riches:"[j] Wealth in the Old Testament seemed to provide some evidence that a man was approved by God. Of course, there were exceptions. There were poor widows who were faithful to God and wealthy men who were ungodly. But in general, wealth and prosperity were signs of God's blessing.

## Conclusion

Many professing Christians are excited about Dave Ramsey's message. His books have been bestsellers, and many would say his message has saved their finances and marriages. But others are not so sure. Does God really intend for New Testament Christians to purposefully accumulate wealth? Are large businesses in our day really a sign of God's blessing? Is the book of Proverbs really the last word in financial teaching?

Dave Ramsey isn't the only one who likes to camp out in the teachings of Proverbs. I have found that Production Pauls, even those in conservative churches, like Proverbs too. One minister and owner of a large company told me recently, "I read a chapter from it every morning. I have learned far more about running a business from the book of Proverbs than from all the business seminars I have attended." Proverbs does a good job of illustrating the importance of sound decision-making in business. Not only that, Proverbs provides a road map for accumulating material wealth. No wonder wealthy businessmen like it. It validates the path they have taken. But before we decide that Proverbs is the last word in Kingdom-focused living, we need to investigate further. What does the New Testament teach? What did Jesus Himself say on this topic?

---

[i] Proverbs 10:15
[j] Proverbs 14:24

# *Business and Jesus* 9

Throughout history the Jewish people have been famous for their business acumen. Probably no people group is better known for skills in business and commerce. When Jesus taught the message we call the Sermon on the Mount, I don't think His listeners were expecting a lesson on finances. Yet Jesus dove right into the topics of wealth and possessions, and I think it is safe to say that, regardless of their financial status, everyone was surprised at His message.

### What Is Jesus' Message?

In the last chapter we looked at what the book of Proverbs has to say regarding business and wealth. The Jewish listeners had heard these teachings all their lives. As we look at a summary of what Jesus had to say, consider how shocking His message would have been.

- **Lacking common sense.** One of the first attributes we see in Jesus' message on economics is an apparent lack of what we call common sense. Notice these words: "Give to him that asketh of thee, and from him that would borrow of thee turn not thou away."[a] Does that sound like common sense to you? Have you ever read anything like this in a "how to run a successful business" book or heard anything like this promoted in a business seminar? What about this one? "And if ye lend to them of whom ye hope to receive, what thank have ye? For sinners also lend to sinners, to receive

---

[a] Matthew 5:42

as much again. But love ye your enemies, and do good, and lend, hoping for nothing again."[b] Can you imagine a bank or credit union operating like this? These statements seem to fly in the face of common sense. I wonder what expressions were on the faces looking back at Jesus that day. Can't you imagine the thoughts racing through the minds of the successful businessmen? *That's foolishness! If I actually did that, what would happen to my business?*

If we're honest, we have had the same thoughts.

- **Self-denial is encouraged.** Our natural tendency has always been to look out for number one. Self-preservation is a normal human focus. Here again the teachings of Jesus are revolutionary. "And as ye would that men should do to you, do ye also to them likewise."[c] Can't you see the wealthy storeowner scratching his head on this one? His goal had always been to convince people they needed his product. Wasn't that what a good salesman was supposed to do? But Jesus is saying that instead of selfishly trying to increase sales to maximize profits, the storeowner should look at transactions from the buyer's point of view. This was a new thought!

  Perhaps a building contractor who was competitively bidding on a project heard Jesus' statement. If he discovered some way he could do the project more efficiently, should he share this information with his competitors who were also bidding on the job? How could a man successfully run a business if he operated like that?

- **Prosperity is a great danger and potential snare.** "Woe unto you that are rich!" Jesus said. "Ye have received your consolation."[d] I suspect the prosperous businessmen were a little shocked by this statement. They weren't used to being reprimanded. After all, they were the industrious

---

[b] Luke 6:34, 35
[c] Luke 6:31
[d] Luke 6:24

ones, the ones people came to when they had a need. They had always looked up to wealthy patriarchs like Job, David, and Solomon. They may have imagined themselves to be modern-day Abrahams, known for their extensive holdings.

Jesus addressed prosperity repeatedly, and His message was consistent: Earthly wealth is a great danger and a potential snare to man. Later in His ministry He again warned against wealth. "How hardly shall they that have riches enter into the kingdom of God! For it is easier for a camel to go through a needle's eye, than for a rich man to enter into the kingdom of God."[e] This saying was so radically different that even the disciples, who were mostly poor men, were shocked. The Bible says they were "exceedingly amazed."[f] This was not the message they had been hearing from their culture or from the rabbi in the synagogue. This was entirely new!

- **Material poverty is a place of potential blessing.** "And he lifted up his eyes on his disciples, and said, Blessed be ye poor: for yours is the kingdom of God."[g] And then, lest anyone be uncertain of what He was saying, Jesus continued, "Blessed are ye that hunger now: for ye shall be filled."[h] If anyone in the crowd hadn't been surprised yet, this statement would surely have done it. The poor and hungry are blessed? What was that supposed to mean? While we want to be careful when interpreting the teachings of Jesus, I think we can say with confidence that God doesn't take pleasure in seeing people go hungry. Just a few chapters later we find Jesus so concerned about His hungry followers that He performed a miracle so they could eat. Rather, in speaking of the poor and hungry, Jesus was exposing one of the snares of earthly wealth. Riches cause us to forget God and depend

[e] Luke 18:24, 25
[f] Matthew 19:25
[g] Luke 6:20
[h] Luke 6:21

less on Him. Where a rich man depends on his wealth for deliverance in time of trouble, a poor man tends to turn to God. For this reason, material poverty is a place of potential spiritual blessing.

- **Worrying about the future is discouraged.** "Therefore I say unto you, Take no thought for your life, what ye shall eat, or what ye shall drink; nor yet for your body, what ye shall put on. Is not the life more than meat, and the body than raiment? Behold the fowls of the air: for they sow not, neither do they reap, nor gather into barns; yet your heavenly Father feedeth them. Are ye not much better than they?"[i] Businessmen are notorious for planning, plotting, and trying to peer into the future. Almost every financial seminar devotes part of the lecture to planning. Was Jesus really saying not to even think about the future? Was He contradicting His teaching on the importance of sitting down and counting the cost before starting a building project?[j] I don't think so. Instead, I believe He was teaching the foolishness of worrying about the future. The English Standard Version of the Bible says: "Therefore I tell you, do not be anxious about your life, what you will eat or what you will drink, nor about your body, what you will put on."[k]

    Maybe we cross that line in business, and perhaps the larger the business the greater the tendency. I have repeatedly found myself lying in bed working through some business challenge, worrying what might happen if a bid was too low (or too high), or anxiously planning for an upcoming meeting with a disgruntled customer. We justify this anxiousness as part of normal business management. But the message of Jesus is that we are to release our fears of the future and turn this anxiety over to Him. This allows us to keep our focus where it needs to be.

[i] Matthew 6:25, 26
[j] Luke 14:28–30
[k] Matthew 6:25 (ESV)

- **Storing in unsecured places is condemned.** "Lay not up for yourselves treasures upon earth, where moth and rust doth corrupt, and where thieves break through and steal."[l] This revolutionary statement surely raised some eyebrows, and it is a message we too quickly gloss over. We hurriedly come up with all kinds of rationale for why it is important to save for the future. But why would Jesus have spoken these words if He didn't want us to obey them? Couldn't He have worded it a little differently? Our Father doesn't intend for His children to trust in earthly treasure, and Jesus goes on to say that "where your treasure is, there will your heart be also." A man who has stockpiled treasure on earth will find his mind swiftly going there when difficulty comes. Man cannot separate his treasure from his heart. But Jesus taught that another problem exists with accumulating and storing material wealth on earth—there aren't any safe locations.

If we're not supposed to store up treasures on earth because it isn't safe, what are we supposed to do? Where should a man stockpile his wealth?

Jesus didn't leave us without answers to these questions. He went on to say, "But lay up for yourselves treasures in heaven, where neither moth nor rust doth corrupt, and where thieves do not break through nor steal."[m] In Luke 12 Jesus gives more detailed instructions, telling us exactly how to invest our wealth. "Sell that you have, and give alms; provide yourselves bags which wax not old, a treasure in the heavens that faileth not, where no thief approacheth, neither moth corrupteth."[n]

If you want to be absolutely sure you are investing your money in a secure location, give it to the poor. Jesus gave the same message to another businessman one day, and it didn't go over very well. We know him as the rich young

---

[l] Matthew 6:19

[m] Matthew 6:20

[n] Luke 12:33

ruler. Jesus told him, "If thou wilt be perfect, go and sell that thou hast, and give to the poor, and thou shalt have treasure in heaven: and come and follow me."° This man had difficulty with Jesus' teaching, and many of us do too. We, like him, would like to keep our hands on our treasure while ensuring its safety at the same time. But Jesus was crystal clear. There isn't a place on earth outside the risk of loss from moth, rust, or thieves. God wants His resources stored in a safe location.

## Conclusion

Jesus didn't leave us very many words. His total public ministry only spanned a few years. Yet centuries have passed and we still wrestle with His teachings. His words reach down into the recesses of our hearts (and wallets), and we can't help but wonder why He didn't use a little softer wording here or a little more explanation there. Did He really intend that businesses try to apply His teachings and operate using His message? Could a business even survive doing this?

If you are involved in business and are a Bible reader, these questions have gone through your mind. And if you are serious about following Jesus, you must answer them. But before we dive into whether or not Jesus would go broke if He tried running a business in America, we need to take a closer look at the book of Proverbs and the teachings of Jesus. Is it possible to reconcile the differences in their messages?

---

° Matthew 19:21

# *Reconciling Proverbs and Jesus* | 10

If we are honest, we must admit there are major differences between Proverbs and the teachings of Jesus. The overriding message in Proverbs is that a wise man works hard, plans ahead, saves for the future, is honest in his business dealings, and over time discovers that God's ways work. A man who continues down this path will eventually enjoy material prosperity, which is evidence that he has been following God's common-sense instructions.

In contrast, Jesus repeatedly teaches the blessing of being poor and the foolishness of focusing on material things. He reminds us that material wealth is a great snare in a man's life, and He emphasizes how superior unseen and eternal treasures are compared to temporal material wealth. If we do accumulate earthly wealth, we are to sell it and give it to the poor. In other words, we need to exchange earthly treasure as quickly as possible for the wealth that is eternal.

Christian financial counselors and business planners use both the teachings of Jesus and the book of Proverbs. There is nothing wrong with this. But they (and we) need to be careful in reconciling their differences.

I am concerned when Christian financial counselors treat Proverbs and the words of Jesus equally in their teaching and writing. But we don't need to look outside our conservative churches to find this. Most of us have been guilty of this at some point in our lives. If we want to emphasize the importance of giving or putting God first in our lives, we might use a teaching of Jesus like, "Seek ye first the kingdom of God, and his righteousness, and all these things shall be added unto you."[a] But if we want to teach how to accumulate wealth, the importance of defending and protecting possessions against loss, or

> **The Bible becomes a big pool of verses, and we dip in and find the passage that says what we want.**

the many ways financial prosperity can be a blessing in our lives (as if we need to be taught), we go to Proverbs. The Bible becomes a big pool of verses, and we dip in and find the passage that says what we want.

## Complete Honesty

As we try to reconcile the differences between Jesus' teachings and Proverbs, we must first be honest about our goals. What am I really after? Am I a Production Paul with an overriding goal to have a large business and be successful by the world's standards? Or am I a Servant Sam who has struggled financially and is frustrated by professing Christians who own large businesses and place too much emphasis on working hard to get ahead? Maybe I would like to find passages denouncing wealth so that I can show those Production Pauls their error.

Whatever we are after, there are verses that can provide justification—or ammunition. So as we proceed, let's stop for a moment and analyze our motives. Men who study the Word of God usually find what they are searching for.

## The Book of Proverbs

It is essential to give consideration to context. The book of Proverbs is a collection of general truths and observations about our world. For example, we are told in Proverbs, "Whoso findeth a wife findeth a good thing."[b] Is this always true? Most of us can think of a man who found a wife who wasn't a blessing to him at all. Yet there is an overriding truth in this verse. Most of us have found our wives to be great blessings in our lives. This statement is a general observation about life.

---

[a] Matthew 6:33
[b] Proverbs 18:22

Think about this verse: "A soft answer turneth away wrath."[c] Does it always? Jesus responded very kindly to His accusers, but they crucified Him anyway. Most of us have experienced situations where we received wrath in spite of our soft answers. But, again, we understand the general truth in this verse. Those who answer with kindness instead of harshness tend to defuse angry confrontations.

The book of Proverbs is full of these kinds of observations. So what should we do with them? Are we to conclude that the book is untrustworthy since some of the statements do not apply to all situations? As we search for God's will concerning business, should we avoid the teachings of Proverbs?

Recently I met a Servant Sam who had come to this conclusion. Since the book of Proverbs is part of the Old Testament, in his estimation its counsel on wealth should be regarded the same way as God's promises regarding material blessing in Deuteronomy. Since the message of Proverbs is different than Jesus' message, its teachings are no longer in effect and should not be used today.

I do not believe this is correct. Proverbs contains much practical advice that still applies today. But as with all teachings found in the Old Testament, we need to be careful how we apply them.

Proverbs teaches us how to make the material world work for us. It is the operating manual provided by the Manufacturer Himself. Men throughout the ages have applied its teachings to their lives, and many have become financially successful. These principles still work and are still true thousands of years after they were first penned. The book of Proverbs contains the formula for material success, and many men have found provision for their natural needs by following its teachings.

Because it is the operating manual for the material world, the principles taught in Proverbs work regardless of your religion. Japan is not known for following the Bible, yet is a a wealthy country. How can this be? Because its people have unknowingly lived out much of the message of Proverbs. Remember, this book contains observations of what works within the material world, and these principles are universal.

---

[c] Proverbs 15:1

Japan has a strong work ethic, is known to be diligent in business, and historically has had one of the highest personal savings rates in the world. Though the average Japanese person may not be aware of the source, these foundational values from Scripture have made the country successful financially.

### The Message of Jesus

But Jesus brought a different message. He didn't give business seminars or lectures on how people could increase their earthly wealth. If you go to His teachings hoping to find pointers on increasing business revenue, you won't find much, because that wasn't His mission. He introduced an eternal Kingdom and challenged us to aim higher than silver and gold. He taught that we should make every decision from an eternal perspective. He said a man who had nothing at the end of his life but earthly possessions was a fool. With authoritative teaching and powerful illustrations He showed us how to look at this material life in a radically different way.

Although His focus and perspective on wealth was different from Proverbs, note that Jesus never suggested that the truths in Proverbs are no longer valid. He didn't say, "Ye have heard it hath been said, 'He that tilleth his land shall have plenty of bread.' But I say unto you, don't get up so early to work in the field. Relax, God knows you need food and will bring it to you." Jesus didn't say it was impossible to accumulate earthly wealth by heeding Proverbs. He just taught that earthly wealth wasn't worth accumulating.

A central theme runs throughout Jesus' teachings regarding money and possessions: everything around us will soon be worthless. And since that day is quickly approaching, a wise man will begin looking at life, money, and possessions from an eternal perspective. Jesus wasn't saying that a good work ethic, saving for known expenses, or being diligent in our business decisions wasn't good. But He was saying that a man can do all of this and still be bankrupt at the end of life. Actually, the author of Proverbs also hinted at this truth. Addressing the foolishness of focusing only on material wealth, the writer said, "There is that maketh himself rich, yet hath nothing: there is that maketh himself poor, yet hath great riches."[d] Even in the Old Testament there was a basic understanding that earthly wealth alone was insufficient, and Jesus persistently emphasized the folly of having an earthbound foundational vision.

Most of us have grown up listening to the Sermon on the Mount. We hear the minister talk about what Jesus said, we discuss and try to understand what He really meant, and we memorize many of the passages. But remember, Jesus was talking to people who had been raised on the book of Proverbs and the Mosaic Law. I don't think we can comprehend the powerful impact His teachings had when they were first spoken. Imagine growing up being taught that God blesses materially those who are faithful to Him. And then Jesus comes along saying it is easier for a camel to go through the eye of a needle than for a rich man to enter into the Kingdom of God. No wonder it says the disciples were astonished. We would have been just as shocked as they were!

### Reconciling Proverbs and Jesus

So what are we to do with the different focus and message? And how are we to apply these differences in our occupations? Although Proverbs and the teachings of Jesus have a different purpose and focus, they do not contradict each other. In fact, both will be essential if you have a vision for operating a Kingdom-focused business. Let's look at how both Proverbs and the teachings of Jesus have powerful roles to play in your business.

- **Proverbs provides the how, Jesus the why.** Proverbs tells

---

[d] Proverbs 13:7

us how to produce income, and the teachings of Jesus tell us why. Proverbs provides the tools to make the material world work for us. We learn that it is important to get out of bed in the morning, that we need be out in the field/workplace to survive, and that we must give thought to business planning. In the New Testament we discover *why* God wants us to be involved in these activities. We are to use money to provide for our families,[e] assist the fatherless and widows,[f] and send aid to needy believers in other parts of the world.[g] None of this is possible without industry, and nothing out there surpasses Proverbs in teaching how to make business profitable. But what is the purpose behind this production and profit? Proverbs teaches how, and Jesus taught us why.

- **Money can be useful in furthering the Kingdom.** In some ways it would have been easier if Jesus had just told us to stay away from money. Sometimes I see young people taking this position out of reaction. But Jesus didn't say this. In fact, He taught that, as dangerous as money is, it can be useful in the Kingdom. One of the most lengthy and difficult parables Jesus told was the story of the unjust steward.[h] Men have wrestled through the years to understand why Jesus would use the account of an unrighteous man to illustrate a godly concept. But the concluding message is clear. While we are not to serve money, it can be useful in furthering the Kingdom of God. Paul picked up this theme in his letter to the church at Ephesus when he encouraged them to earn money so they would "have to give to him that needeth."[i]

- **Surrender what is right and fair.** Proverbs describes what is right and fair and has many teachings regarding cause

---

[e] 1 Timothy 5:8

[f] James 2:27

[g] 2 Corinthians 8:14

[h] Luke 16:1–12

[i] Ephesians 4:28

and effect. If you do certain things, you can expect certain results. It describes what is just and reasonable, and every business owner should be familiar with it. But the teachings of Jesus take us far beyond the pursuit of what is right and fair. They call us to lay down our personal rights—to *not* insist on receiving what may be fair and equitable, and to consider each business transaction from the other person's perspective. Jesus doesn't disagree with the teachings in Proverbs describing fair treatment. He just taught us not to insist on it.

- **Both agree that wealth is to be accumulated.** Both Proverbs and the teachings of Jesus encourage accumulation of wealth. But while Proverbs primarily focuses on the blessings that come from accumulating temporal wealth,[j] Jesus' teachings emphasize another kind of treasure and a different place to save. In contrast to temporal wealth, which is subject to moth, rust, and thieves, Jesus reveals a savings account surpassing any security measures man can provide.[k] He says we can direct-deposit into this heavenly account now. Imagine that! You can almost sense the excitement in Jesus' voice as He urges His listeners, "Sell that ye have, and give alms; provide yourselves bags which wax not old, a treasure in the heavens that faileth not, where no thief approacheth, neither moth corrupteth."[l] Business owners are interested in return on investment. There is no greater risk-free investment being offered today, and wise business owners will shift their assets to this heavenly account as quickly as possible.

## Conclusion

The book of Proverbs contains the universal building blocks for providing for our families. I can think of no better resource for a young

---

[j] Proverbs 14:24

[k] Matthew 6:19

[l] Luke 12:33

man who wants to understand how to make the material world work for him. It will teach him to work hard and plan ahead, and it will provide the principles required for successful business operation. Everyone should become familiar with its teachings. But in the middle of all our hustle and bustle, it is essential to stop and ask *why* diligence and a good work ethic are so important. Proverbs and the teachings of Jesus are intended to complement each other.

The natural entrepreneur loves logic, challenge, production, and common sense, and the business world naturally rewards the man who pursues these attributes. Consequently, Christians who enjoy business can become enamored with the Biblical truths in Proverbs and give less attention to the call of Jesus. Beware! A man who lives only by the teachings of Proverbs can die a fool![m]

> A man who lives only by the teachings of Proverbs can die a fool!

It is easy for most businessmen to wrap their minds around the common-sense teachings of Proverbs. But what about the teachings of Jesus and the apostles? Paul reiterated Jesus' view on seeking wealth when he told the church at Corinth, "Let no man seek his own, but every man another's wealth."[n] How can a man operate a profitable business while doing this?

---

[m] Luke 12:21
[n] 1 Corinthians 10:24

# *Would Jesus Go Broke?*  |  11

When we choose to follow Jesus, we relinquish our right to earthly wealth, possibly even what is right and fair, and live instead for Him and His Kingdom. Yet as wonderful as that may sound, the man who chooses to live for eternity still needs to provide for his family. So are the teachings of Jesus compatible with the modern business world? Or to put it more bluntly, if Jesus tried to operate a business in the dog-eat-dog business environment of our day, would He go broke? Can enterprises be profitable using Jesus' business model?

Before answering this question, let's look at some basic principles we find in the teachings of Jesus:

- **The Kingdom of God must be primary.** Jesus was clear that a man must first seek the Kingdom of God.[a] This foundational truth is easily forgotten amidst the constant stress and pressure of business life, and we need to be reminded often. Following Jesus is to be first, and every other passion and pursuit is to be relegated to a subservient position. "Whosoever he be of you who forsaketh not all that he hath," Jesus said, "he cannot be my disciple."[b] Jesus calls us to surrender everything and follow Him, even if it means abandoning our family relationships. Since Jesus calls us to place our families on the altar, our businesses must be placed there as well.

---

[a] Matthew 6:33
[b] Luke 14:33

The New Testament commands us to labor and provide for our families.[c] But it is tempting to hide business ambition behind this. God has given men a desire to make things work—an inner craving to produce and provide. This is good and normal, and we become concerned when this is absent in a man's life. But this inner desire, which God meant for good, becomes a snare when outside the Lordship of Jesus Christ. We need to daily reexamine our values. Jesus insinuated that one soul has more worth than the entire world.[d] Do I really believe this? Would someone watching my business transactions each day say I believe it? The Kingdom of God must be primary in our lives, and we need to be called back daily to this truth.

- **Increase is of God.** Several years ago I was asked to speak to a group of pastors in Ukraine about finances. Afterward, a pastor in the back of the room stood and asked, "Can you show me a verse in the Bible that tells us it is right for a business to make a profit on a sale?" I have been asked many questions after financial seminars, but this was a new one! Acceptable to make a profit in business? You will never hear that question in North America. To appreciate the question, we must understand the setting. These pastors had been raised under communism. The government was supposed to supply all their needs, though it rarely did. The only individuals involved in commerce were criminals operating in the black market. These undercover merchants preyed on the fact that many lacked daily necessities, and they charged exorbitant prices for their products. Consequently, the Ukrainian church had developed a belief that selling a product for more than you had paid for it was wrong.

  Jesus didn't teach that it was wrong for a man to earn a profit. In fact, all through His teachings you find the

---

[c] 1 Timothy 5:8
[d] Matthew 16:26

opposite. Many of His teachings, miracles, and even the natural world He created demonstrate that profit or increase is of God. How many of us would plant one seed of corn if we knew at harvest time we would only get one in return? Multiplication is a basic principle in nature. In one parable we find a man upbraided for not at least putting his money in the bank to earn interest. In the same account men were praised for multiplying the investment that had been entrusted to them. Jesus multiplied the five loaves and two fishes and caused the disciples' nets to break from the huge catch of fish. Jesus was not opposed to increase. He wants us to understand that increase is of God.

Sometimes we react to others' selfish use of their profits, and we develop improper conclusions. Like the Ukrainian pastor, we become so intent on avoiding one ditch that we end up in another. God intends that our fields and factories produce a profit. As those profits increase, so does our responsibility as stewards of what the Lord has given us to manage. "For unto whomsoever much is given, of him shall be much required."[e]

- **We are to seek the good of others.** Early in Jesus' ministry He said, "As ye would that men should do to you, do ye also to them likewise."[f] We have our children memorize this principle and rightly tell them that living it out will help them avoid many squabbles with their playmates. But how do we apply it in business?

  While this teaching can be difficult to live out, it will be easier if our first priority is to have a Kingdom-focused business. Go back to the first point: The Kingdom of God must be primary. The concept of seeking the good of others is one of the Biblical principles most lacking in Christian businesses today. As mentioned earlier, profit itself is not wrong. But

---

[e] Luke 12:48
[f] Luke 6:31

neither is profit to be the only purpose in our businesses. Recently I went to a local hardware store to buy a tube of silicone. I took it up to the counter, and the clerk informed me that it would cost me about four dollars. I had four dollars in my pocket.

I would have liked to keep my money, but at that moment I  wanted that silicone more than I wanted the four dollars. And the hardware store wanted my four dollars more than it wanted that tube of silicone. The exchange was made, and both of us were happy as we parted. That is healthy commerce.

But why did that tube of silicone cost four dollars? If that business operates like most businesses, they charged four dollars because they thought that was the highest price I would be willing to pay for it. The price is based on a market-based equilibrium, with the seller closely calculating how he can extract the most money from the buyer and produce the most income. This is how the capitalistic business culture generally works. But a Kingdom-focused business will use more than potential profits to determine pricing. We also want to ensure that the other person is receiving what he needs in the exchange.

I can think of many Christian businessmen who exemplify this virtue—men I do business with who always give a little more, charge a little less, or in some way exceed my expectations. I come to them with a picture in my mind of what I want to receive and what it should cost, and somehow they manage to provide more for less.

Growing up, I used to hear stories about a farmer named Alvin. It was well known in his community that if you were doing business with Alvin you needed to keep your eye on him. If you bought hay, you'd better watch the tally. He seemed to find ways to slip extra bales in when you weren't looking. I remember hearing men tell of sharecropping with him. Alvin had all kinds of creative ways to make sure they got the best end of a deal. Alvin has been gone for many years, yet people still talk about him. I believe a healthy church or community should be full of people like this, each trying to secretly bless the other as they interact and transact business. Paul calls this being a cheerful (Greek: hilarious) giver, and I like to imagine church communities filled with people like Alvin.[g]

Earlier we said that increase is of God. A follower of Jesus, however, will not base every decision solely on how it will affect him, his company, or his bottom line. He will also give thought to what is best for the other person. The Apostle Paul told the church at Corinth, "Let no man seek his own, but every man another's wealth."[h] A Kingdom-focused businessman will be driven by more than just potential income. He will also aim to bless the other person in every transaction.

- **Our activities are to glorify God.** "Let your light so shine before men," Jesus said, "that they may see your good works, and glorify your Father which is in heaven."[i] Live your life and conduct all your activities in such a way that those looking on will be inspired to turn toward God. This simple command should permeate all our business activities.

One time when I was working on a construction site, I came into a room just as the general contractor had left. The owner was lingering in the room after their meeting, staring out a window at the receding figure of the contractor. Pointing toward the contractor, he turned to me and said

---

[g] 2 Corinthians 9:7
[h] 1 Corinthians 10:24
[i] Matthew 5:16

with emotion, "That man is the closest imitation of Jesus Christ I have ever met."

I have no idea what those two men had been discussing. But whatever had occurred, that Christian contractor had conducted himself in such a Christ-like manner that this man was astonished. Living out what Jesus taught will impact how we treat our customers, respond to vendors, and fulfill our contracts. It will cause us to speak, act, and respond differently in daily life. And the man who is dedicated to following Jesus in business will find himself basing every decision on whether or not it glorifies his Father in heaven.

- **God still cares about "all these things."** A cursory read of the teachings of Jesus might cause you to conclude that God no longer blesses materially—that in the Old Testament God blessed His people with earthly things, but now His only blessings are spiritual. While it is true that Jesus warned against wealth, taught that it would be extremely difficult for a rich man to enter heaven, and cautioned us not to be anxious about our physical needs, it is important to remember that material provision still comes from God. After giving strong admonition not to worry about what we will eat, drink, or wear, Jesus said, "But seek ye first the kingdom of God, and his righteousness; and all these things shall be added unto you."[j] God hasn't forgotten about our natural needs. He made us and understands that we need food and clothing to survive.

  This verse isn't saying that God will supply our growing list of wants. But it is a promise that He will be with us and provide for our needs. Many believers throughout history have been called to live in poverty, and many today still live in difficult conditions simply because they have chosen to follow Jesus. I met a young girl in Indonesia who was raised Muslim, and her choice to follow Jesus had disrupted her

---

[j] Matthew 6:33

entire life. When I met her, she was trying to find some community where no one would recognize her, because her immediate family would kill her if she was found. She wasn't sure how she was going to survive and was concerned about physical provision. But God is well able to provide, and Jesus cares about these situations. "Verily I say unto you, There is no man that hath left house, or brethren, or sisters, or father, or mother, or wife, or children, or lands, for my sake, and the gospel's, but he shall receive an hundredfold now in this time, houses, and brethren, and sisters, and mothers, and children, and lands, with persecutions; and in the world to come eternal life."[k]

Many believers in restricted countries could attest to the truth of this promise. They have walked away from all earthly resources and relationships only to find new friends, open doors to homes, and meals around tables with people God has provided for them. So let's follow Jesus in faith. Let's place our business decisions in His care. He knows we have material needs and is well able to provide all these physical things.

Is it possible to follow Jesus and be financially successful? I have observed many Christians who apply His teachings daily in their businesses. They are public demonstrations that Jesus' teachings are not incompatible with their occupations. And the problems they experience and the ways they respond provide excellent opportunities to demonstrate powerful truths.

**Business Dilemmas**

William owned a small construction company. A man who enjoyed hunting big game around the globe asked him to construct a building to show off his trophy animals. William began the project, and everything was going well. The site work was finished and the concrete slab poured when small cracks began developing all over the slab. The

---

[k] Mark 10:29, 30

owner asked William about these fissures, and he contacted the concrete contractor and the ready-mix supplier in an effort to determine the problem.

The concrete contractor and supplier came to a meeting, but both immediately pointed fingers at the other. One said the concrete hadn't been finished correctly, and the other insisted the product had been deficient from the batch plant. At the conclusion of the meeting, nothing had been decided. Everyone proclaimed his innocence, and the concrete was still cracked. Since the concrete wasn't structural and would be covered with carpet, both said the issue wasn't that important anyway.

Within a few days William received another call from the owner, who wasn't happy about the situation. He agreed that these tiny cracks in the concrete were not very important, but he didn't like that these men had provided an inferior product yet expected him to pay the full price. So the owner stated that, since William was the general contractor, he was going to sue him to get even with the ready-mix supplier and the concrete contractor.

William, more than anything else, wanted his business to glorify God. As he talked to the owner, he shared his faith in Christ and his desire to be known for honesty and integrity. He described the reproach that involvement in a public lawsuit might have on his Christian witness in the community. But none of this moved the owner. He had paid good money for this concrete and couldn't stand the thought of the supplier and contractor getting off free.

William would have loved to just refund part of what the owner had paid, but he had a young family and few financial resources to draw from, so he made a proposal. He asked the owner if there was something he could do for him personally to resolve the situation, maybe something extra on the building he could do free of charge. The owner thought about this and finally said there was. He needed to build a small pump house, and if William would construct this for him at no charge, he would be satisfied. So that's what William did. The next Saturday found him over at the project site early in the morning working on the pump house.

This went on for several Saturdays. One morning the owner stopped by to see how things were going. He talked to William for a while and then exclaimed, "William, this isn't right! You are out here working for nothing, and the men who created this problem are not paying a thing! This isn't fair, and the concrete problem isn't that big a deal anyway. When you get done building this, I want you to send me a bill for your time and the materials."

William's primary desire was that the Lord would be glorified by his business dealings, and he was willing to lose money to make this happen. If he had shown any resistance, there would have been court costs, and the owner could have made William's life miserable for the duration of the project. But by following Jesus and staying true to his vision of living for the Kingdom, he not only kept his Christian witness, but he also built a strong relationship with the owner. As an added blessing, he even got paid for his efforts.

It is amazing how often God materially blesses individuals who choose to take the path of Jesus. But will situations always turn out like William's? Of course not. Many business owners have sustained huge losses by choosing to follow Jesus' teachings.

Jack Phillips is the owner of Masterpiece Cakeshop in Lakewood, Colorado. Phillips doesn't believe gay marriage is Biblical, so he refused to bake a wedding cake for David Mullins and Charlie Craig. Consequently, these two men took Jack Phillips to court, claiming discrimination against their sexual orientation. Phillips testified that he would be willing to sell cupcakes for a birthday party for someone who is gay, but said, "I don't want to participate in a same-sex wedding."[1] The court ruled against Phillips. As a result, he has chosen to stop making wedding cakes. This will result in a huge loss of revenue and profits.

### Conclusion

William ended up gaining financially because of his decision to follow Jesus. But we need to understand that this will not always be the result. In Paul's letter to the church at Corinth, he inferred that there will be times when choosing to follow Jesus will mean we are defrauded and taken advantage of.[1] When we choose to follow Jesus, we need to

---

[1] 1 Corinthians 6:7

understand this possibility.

Could Jesus be successful as a businessman in our world? Absolutely! His teachings are not incompatible with business. Many could testify how His teachings have helped them resolve conflicts with customers, develop an extremely loyal customer base, and even receive payment on overdue bills. But in asking this question we must reexamine our definition of success. If our primary motive is large profits, there is little in the New Testament that guarantees increased income to the Christian. But if our primary desire is to provide for our families, assist those in need, and portray Christ to the world through our businesses, we can move forward in confidence. Jesus is calling more businessmen today to place their personal business ambitions on the altar and make their first priority to be about their Father's business.

# PART THREE

## *The Sacred and the Secular*

# *Theological Gymnastics* | 12

A s we read the accounts of early believers in the book of Acts and on through the writings of the first few hundred years of Christianity, there can be no doubt: those who were called Christians were followers of Jesus in everyday life. They read His words, applied His teachings, and attempted to imitate His life with their own. Choosing to be a Christian was a serious step, compounded in many places by intense persecution. Only those who were committed to a radical change in life were willing to take that step.

But in the years following Constantine, something drastically different began to occur. Membership in the church became territorial. Now you were known as a Christian simply due to the country or province you were born into. If the government decided your region was to be Christian, then everyone living within that geographical area became known as Christian. This created a real problem for church leaders. What was a leader supposed to do when a large percentage of the people under his care were called Christians by the government, yet their lives of drunkenness, idolatry, and immorality bore little resemblance to Jesus Christ?

It was no use to dispute what Jesus had taught. His teachings were clear. Neither could the church leaders convince themselves that these members were bearing godly fruit. The evidence against them was too conclusive. It seemed there were only two options. Either lower God's standard for holiness or call the people up higher. But since changing the written Word isn't easy to do, and forcibly changing men's hearts is even harder, theologians like Augustine came up with an ingenious third option.

## The Third Option

The solution? Just separate a man's obedience to God from his standing with Him. Men like Augustine taught that what you believed about Jesus was much more important than literally living out His teachings. In describing how a man could go to war while still being obedient to Jesus, Augustine said that loving your enemies is not a "bodily action, but an inward disposition."[1] In other words, it is acceptable to kill your enemy as long as you are loving him while doing it, and what is going on in the mind is of far greater importance than what you see demonstrated in the life.

The fruit of this erroneous Augustinian doctrine lives on today. It isn't uncommon—in fact, one could argue that it has become normal—to find a man living in open disobedience to the teachings of Jesus, yet believing he is in good standing with God. But notice how this was done. Theologians didn't alter the fact that God will someday doom many to hell. Neither did they say that God doesn't want holiness. Instead, they manufactured a theology that kept a man out of hell without holiness. Now, through theological gymnastics, a man could be holy before God without living a holy life before men.

But before we are too hard on these theologians, is it possible that we have accomplished a similar feat with regard to our view of wealth and business? We read the teachings of Jesus regarding money and working with others, and we agree His way is best. We can explain in a Bible study or a sermon why the path of Jesus is superior. But we get out into the world of business, and suddenly it looks almost impossible to literally apply the teachings of Jesus. We sit in our office chairs and find ourselves in a similar dilemma to that of the church leaders struggling with a territorial church. We can't change the teachings of Jesus, and though we wouldn't admit it, we really can't imagine Jesus fitting into our business environment. Yet we have to provide for our families. So we subconsciously separate our business from our spiritual life to make it all work.

## The Conflict Between Kingdoms

We commonly hear that the secular capitalist business world is built upon greed and selfishness. While some might disagree, arguing that other economic models are even worse, there is some truth in this statement. This doesn't mean everyone buying and selling within this system is greedy, but the success of each enterprise rests on the owner looking after his own interests. We in the Western world have grown up subconsciously being taught that each person has to look out for number one. Looking out for ourselves and pursuing financial success are normal behaviors within our economic model.

Donald Trump, one of America's most outspoken successful businessmen, has promoted this concept. Perhaps nothing reveals more about his perspective on business than his famous slogan, "It's not whether you win or lose, but whether you win!" Though Donald Trump may be brasher and bolder than most, his statement reveals a conviction many have come to believe: business is a competitive game, and every businessman is in a battle against every other. Consequently, the materialistic capitalist ventures forth each day knowing that if he is going to succeed, he must look out for his own best interests.

### Oil and Water

Consequently, those of us who are following Jesus and involved in business have a huge problem. His teachings are in direct opposition to our self-centered business culture. You can't just make a few adjustments to Jesus' teachings to make them compatible with common business practices. Like oil and water, they just won't mix, regardless how hard we stir. Lending without hoping for anything in return, seeking the wealth of others, and doing to our competitors and customers as we would want them to do to us—how are we to mix these concepts with business?

These are two diametrically opposed ways of looking at life—two completely different cultures. The one is a culture of self-centeredness, always looking at each event or transaction in light of how it will affect the bottom line. Maybe we could call this a "business culture."

The other is centered on the wellbeing of the other person—focusing on the needs of others and reaching out to the lost, the needy, and the struggling. Perhaps we could call this a "church culture."

Two completely incompatible cultures. They are not going to mix well, so what do we do?

### Business Is Business

Amos is known in his community as a good businessman. He lives a disciplined life, knows how to drive a hard bargain, and has consistently made wise business decisions. He is shrewd in his dealings, and as an employer of many men has little time for the employee who won't put his all into his work. Amos has been successful in business.

Amos is also a minister in his church and is known for helping those who are down and out. Many struggling people come to him, and he helps them financially. On the one hand, Amos can be tightfisted and is known for haggling a vendor down as far as possible. On the other hand, Amos is the first to share when there is a need at church. One of Amos's favorite sayings is, "Business is business."

Understand, Amos would never steal, lie, or cheat people out of what was rightfully theirs. But how he deals with a vendor in the business world and the way he interacts with someone fallen on hard times in his church are radically different. He has learned to operate in completely different ways within these two cultures and can swap mindsets seamlessly.

### You Had Better Be Alert!

Recently I met a man who had moved his small business into an area with a high concentration of conservative churches. He had never lived among Plain People before.

"I assumed when I moved here," he told me, "that these people would be easier to do business with. I wasn't raised in a Christian home, and I thought people who had chosen to live radically different lives in other ways would be less intent on chasing the dollar."

But his experience was just the opposite.

"I was shocked to discover that both vendors and customers from these conservative churches were much harder to do business with than the average American consumer." He went on to say that their vendors could be extremely hard-nosed and focused on getting the highest prices possible for their goods. On the other hand, he had found exactly the opposite when working with the same people as customers. These Plain People were known for driving prices down when buying. "They may claim to be followers of Jesus," he told me, "but they are not thinking about your good. They wouldn't think of telling an outright lie or of walking off without paying. But if you do business with them, you had better be alert!"

I was saddened by what this man shared. Here was a community, presumably wanting to be a light to the world, but instead famous for dickering and not caring about the good of others when doing business. Is this only true of that community? I look at my own life and wonder. I know there have been times when I was more interested in making or saving a few dollars than in the soul of the individual I was doing business with. We find it easier in business to comply with Old Testament laws like not stealing than to fully embrace New Testament concepts like thinking more of others than ourselves.

**Conclusion**

It is clear that the church lost much more than it gained when it chose to separate a man's obedience to God from his standing with Him. Separating obedience from salvation may have assisted theologians who were trying to explain why their parishioners weren't acting like Christians, but it was erroneous doctrine. When a man convinces himself he can be a follower of Jesus without following His teachings, he is deceived, and many will end up in hell due to this doctrinal decep-tion.[a] The long-term damage to the church that followed this theolo-gy is horrific. Millions have embraced this lie, and the church at large is still confused on this issue.

But what about the impact of separating our spiritual lives from our businesses? Might we be involved in theological gymnastics as well? And if so, what kind of damage has this done to our testimony and Christian witness in our communities? What are some of the repercus-sions of separating the secular from the spiritual in our lives?

---

[a] Matthew 25:31–46; Luke 6:46–49

# Sacred or Secular? | 13

"Any of you who would like to devote your life to the Lord and be a missionary, raise your hand." The teacher had been reading mission stories to the class, and now, while the exciting accounts were still on their minds, she was hoping her students would internalize the message. A few students raised their hands while others pondered. All of them enjoyed the thought of traveling to some exotic foreign land to share the Gospel, but most were not prepared to commit. After all, they were only sixth graders. Some lived on dairy farms and assumed they would continue farming when their parents grew older. Others had parents who owned small businesses, and they were looking forward to the day they could help. Most of the young girls assumed they would become mothers and pictured themselves with houses full of children. Many hadn't really given much thought to their occupations or futures. They were just attending school and enjoying childhood.

But the students learned something subconsciously that day. As one of the students told me years later, "We learned that missionaries were the truly devoted ones. The few who raised their hands were the dedicated followers of Jesus, and the rest of us were second class Christians. Real Christians were missionaries!"

## Natural versus Spiritual

All of us compartmentalize our lives. Some things are more important than others. I don't treat a passport the same way I do a piece of scrap paper. But we need to be careful when we try to separate the natural from the spiritual in our lives. Many Christians assume that being involved in business makes one a second-class Christian. We sometimes hear that a person is leaving business to go into full-time ministry. But is that Biblical? Did God really intend that full-time ministry only applies to those living in foreign countries or working for non-profit organizations? Is it possible that God intended business to be a full-time ministry as well? Are the mundane tasks of everyday life reserved exclusively for the unbeliever and uncommitted Christians?

Imagine for a moment that everyone on the planet suddenly became a Christian. Would we no longer need plumbers, architects, cooks, and garbage collectors? If all the people in the world committed to following Jesus, would they all suddenly walk away from their occupations? Admittedly some would and should. But some would be honoring God by continuing to build roads, plant crops, and milk cows. In fact, it would be wrong for all of these people to neglect the work God has placed in their care. God has given different gifts to different people, and that is why we have Production Pauls, Larry Littles, and Servant Sams. In the Old Testament we read of men who were given certain abilities by God and were expected to be involved in specific activities. Chenaniah's job, while David was king, was to teach others how to sing, and the Bible says he was given this job because he was skilled.[a] God had given him a gift in music and expected him to use that ability within His Kingdom.

When it was time to build the tabernacle in the wilderness, God told Moses, "See, I have called by name Bezaleel the son of Uri, the son of Hur, of the tribe of Judah: and I have filled him with the spirit of God, in wisdom, and in understanding, and in knowledge, and in all

[a] 1 Chronicles 15:22

manner of workmanship, to devise cunning works, to work in gold, and in silver, and in brass, and in cutting of stones, to set them, and in carving of timber, to work in all manner of workmanship."[b]

Notice how specific God was. He had a specific task for a particular man and had filled Bezaleel with His Spirit, intending that Bezaleel perform this work. But was his labor sacred or secular? It involved melting down metals, carving chunks of wood, and chipping away at stone. That sounds physical and natural. Would it have been better for Bezaleel to have become more involved in "spiritual" activities like offering incense or going off to tell the Canaanites about God? I think we can safely say it would have been sin for Bezaleel to have ignored the ability God had given him. Regardless how "spiritual" the alternate activity he chose to pursue, God had given him a specific gift and expected him to use it.

Martin Luther is supposed to have said, "The cobbler gives God the highest praise when he makes the finest pair of shoes." While much of Luther's teaching was erroneous, I believe he got this right. God calls men to further the Kingdom of God within their occupations by using the natural gifts He has given them. Let's look at some misconceptions that develop when we start separating the natural from the spiritual.

**Spiritual Activities Have More Value**

We tend to think that reading our Bibles, singing hymns, and attending church are spiritual activities. But are you aware that each of these actions can also be sin? When a life becomes unbalanced, even the things we regard as good and unquestionably spiritual can become sinful. Several years ago a pastor in another country asked if I would go with him to visit a man in his congregation. This man just couldn't seem to hold down a job and provide for his family, and the pastor was searching for answers.

As we walked into the man's home, I noticed a couple of things immediately. First, there was almost no furniture. There was one twin bed, one chair, and a set of bookshelves well stocked with books. Second, an air of despondency hung heavily in the house. This man had a wife

---

[b] Exodus 31:2–5

and several children, but they would hardly look us in the eye. The man told us to sit on the bed, he sat on the only chair, and his wife and children stood along the wall. Looking around this desolate room, I couldn't help but feel sorry for the wife and children.

As we discussed their situation, the real problem became clear. This man spent his time reading his Bible, *Martyr's Mirror,* and Bible commentaries instead of working so his children could eat. He had tried different occupations, but it seemed the job never suited him, and he would return home and once again immerse himself in books. Although he loved to read the Word of God, he was neglecting his family. He viewed himself as a spiritual man because he was involved daily in spiritual activities. But the fact is, he was lazy, trying to hide behind the misconception that "spiritual" activities have more value.

**Constant Guilt**

Paul told the church at Philippi that they should "approve things that are excellent."[c] He didn't want them to make choices and be involved in things that were less than the absolute best. We understand this, and all of us who have a Kingdom-focused vision want to be engaged only in things that are excellent. But if we conclude that "spiritual activities" are more excellent and have more value than taking care of natural things, there are two potential destinations: hunger or guilt.

Thus we shuffle off to work again, nagged by a sense of guilt that we should be spending more time in spiritual activities. But does God want us to feel guilty when sleeping, eating, or working? I don't want to minimize the reality that many of us should be spending more time in the Word, in prayer and fasting, and in helping those in need around us. But God made us with natural needs, and He intends that we expend time and effort in addressing those needs. When we separate the spiritual and natural in our lives, we will struggle with an underlying sense of guilt that God didn't intend.

**Business Becomes a "Necessary Evil"**

Another result of separating the sacred and the spiritual is that business

---

[c] Philippians 1:10

can become a necessary evil. Many of us have at one time or another had problems with our septic systems. Maybe the water backed up in the toilet and we were forced to uncover the septic tank and investigate the problem. Perhaps the tank needed to be pumped out or the leach field dug out. Whatever the remedy, it usually isn't pleasant. I have never met a man who enjoys repairing his septic system or heard of someone heading off on vacation hoping to find an overworked septic system to work on while he is there.

Yet when the water backs up in the toilet, we usually do something. Why? Because we consider the result of ignoring this problem worse than fixing it. As stinky and messy as it is, we know something must be done. We refer to something we don't like, yet know must exist, as a necessary evil, and some people regard business that same way. Rather than seeing the potential blessing business can be to the Kingdom of God, they see it as nothing but a requirement for survival.

**A Different Set of Rules**

When we separate business from our spiritual lives, it also becomes easy to justify a different set of rules. Recently I overheard two businessmen discussing mechanic's liens[d] and whether or not a believer should use them. One of the men said, "Well, I don't think Jesus intends for us to let people treat us like doormats. If we didn't use mechanic's liens, lots of our customers would take advantage of us." Where in the teachings of Jesus would you find support for this statement? Did Jesus leave us an example of always making sure no one took advantage of Him?

**Conclusion**

God has placed a soul, something of extreme value, into our fleshly bodies. This soul of extreme value cries out for more of God. Like the Apostle Paul, we have an inner desire to know Him, and our souls will be satisfied with nothing less. But that isn't all that is going on. While our souls seek more of God, our flesh has needs as well. So we live in this tension between earth and heaven. And as diverse as these two

---

[d] Mechanic's liens provide a legal claim upon property as security against a debt or payment for services or products. It is a legal method of requiring consumers to pay for what they receive, using the law to recover payment for the service or product if they do not pay as agreed.

pulls are, it is little wonder that we have a tendency to separate them.

A.W. Tozer, in describing the difficulty believers have in navigating this sacred/secular struggle, said, "Most Christians are caught in a trap. They cannot get a satisfactory adjustment between the claims of these two worlds. They try to walk the tightrope between two kingdoms and they find no peace in either."[1] The result of this is joyless living. But must we remain strung between these two tensions? Is there a solution to this constant struggle and the resulting tendency to separate? This separation has had a tremendous impact on the message going out of the Christian church. Many have walked away from God due to the hypocrisy of following Jesus in one part of life and following culture in business dealings. We each need to face this honestly. Have you been guilty of this? What kind of testimony and Christian witness is going out of your business? And what message *could* go out?

Let's see what we can learn from the example of Jesus.

# *The Interwoven Life* | 14

The Bible teaches us that God is a Spirit,[a] yet He created us as physical beings. So how should it affect a man when he is indwelt by a spiritual God? Does God expect this man to suddenly begin focusing only on invisible spiritual things? And if so, how can he continue providing for his family?

In the last chapter we looked at our tendency to divide the sacred from the secular and the resulting tension believers find themselves in. God keeps calling us higher, while our human needs keep us grounded. How can we serve God and be fully devoted to Him while occupied with the daily, mundane issues of life? Let's begin by looking at the life of Jesus and how He dealt with this tension between two worlds.

## Jesus' Example

On the one hand we like to think of Jesus as being just like we are. He was tempted with the same earthly allurements, seemed exasperated at times with other people, and even displayed anger when confronted with hypocrisy. In some ways He was the same, yet He was strikingly different. He knew what others were thinking, loved the very kind of people we struggle to appreciate, and lived in this corrupt world without sinning. Just like us, yet radically different! Perhaps even to a greater degree than we do, Jesus had to live with this tension between the heavenly and earthly.

We read very little about Jesus' business life. The Gospel of Mark tells

---

[a] John 4:24

us Jesus was a carpenter,[b] and Justin Martyr, an early Christian apologist in the second century, says Jesus made various wooden farm implements such as plows, yokes, and other tools.[1] Other than this we have little information, though it appears that Jesus worked in carpentry much longer than He labored in public ministry. But we have enough clues from His later life and teachings to get a good picture of how He lived as a man.

First, it is clear that Jesus had to deal with His humanity. Just because He was God didn't mean He wasn't in the flesh. The Gospels tell us that He got tired and had to rest.[c] He struggled with hunger[d] and thirst[e] and exhaustion just as we do. There were times when He couldn't do everything He wanted to do[f] and times He experienced frustration.[g] We read how he headed off to be by Himself upon hearing sad news[h] and desired to just get away from it all when life became stressful.

**A Greater Purpose**

So how did Jesus deal with this dichotomy between the natural and the spiritual, and what motivated His daily choices? I think the answer is found in His own words. Describing His relationship with His Father and how this affected His daily life, Jesus said, "I do always those things that please Him."[i] Jesus ate when He was hungry, drank when thirsty, and slept when tired. He participated in all these natural activities without guilt because He was doing them for a greater purpose. In fact, being human, He couldn't have done the things that pleased His Father without taking part in these physical activities. Yet as He was doing this, He focused on a greater objective than pleasing His flesh. There was always a spiritual purpose in His natural activities.

Some of us have had the opportunity to watch someone use a loom to weave a cloth or tapestry. Various colors of thread are woven into the

---

[b] Mark 6:3

[c] John 4:6

[d] Mark 11:12

[e] John 19:28

[f] Mark 6:5; Matthew 13:58

[g] Matthew 17:17; Mark 3:5

[h] Matthew 14:1–13

[i] John 8:29

loom, the shuttle flies back and forth, and slowly a beautiful product is created. The colorful threads going in are distinct. Maybe there is one spool of red thread, another of blue, and another of yellow. Though each thread is distinctly different going in, when the tapestry is complete, it is difficult to discern their variations. Standing back from a well-constructed tapestry, all you see is the beauty of the overall product. And your mind, instead of going to the differences of the individual threads, will usually dwell on the magnificence of the weaving and the skill of the weaver.

## The Interwoven Life

The life of Jesus was much the same way. His activities were diverse. Sometimes He was taking care of a physical ailment and focusing on natural need, and the next moment He was pointing people to the ultimate significance of the eternal. He lived an interwoven life, and it is hard to separate His spiritual activities from His natural activities.

The Gospel of John relates how Jesus was walking one day, became weary, and sat down on Jacob's well to rest—a natural thing to do. Then He asked a woman at this well to draw some water for Him to drink because He was thirsty. But when Jesus asked this woman for water, was His purpose to take care of His natural needs or to teach her a spiritual lesson? It was both. How can we separate the two?

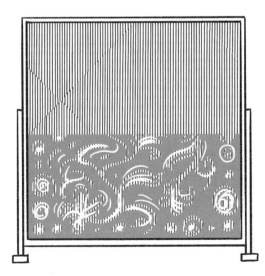

We see this all through Jesus' life. He repeatedly used physical things like seeds, bushel baskets, and the wind to explain spiritual truths. Even as He prepared to leave this earth, He used natural things like bread and wine to illustrate His purpose on earth. As we study His life, we give little thought to which part was physical and which was spiritual. We can't help but admire the beauty of the tapestry and the magnificence of our Creator God! This is true for a simple reason. Whether dealing with daily natural needs or teaching great spiritual truths, Jesus' ultimate goal was that His Father would be glorified.

**Jesus' Life — Our Example**

This should be the goal for every follower of Jesus as well. No matter how mundane our tasks, our goal should be to glorify our Father in heaven. Paul told the church at Colosse, "And whatever ye do in word or deed, do all in the name of the Lord Jesus."[j] Whatever the task, be sure it is done in a way that the Lord Jesus is magnified. In his letter to the church at Corinth, Paul was even more specific. "Whether therefore ye eat, or drink, or whatsoever ye do, do all to the glory of God."[k]

Even eating and drinking? Paul used the most basic of human needs and activities to make a point. A believer in Jesus should be so intent on glorifying God that no part of His daily life is exempt, regardless of how routine that part is. The natural and spiritual threads should be so interwoven that an onlooker can hardly distinguish between them. Rather, he or she should be overcome by the larger beauty the believer's life portrays. An interwoven life produces a tapestry that draws men and women to the beauty of the character of Jesus Christ within.

Just before He went to the cross, Jesus prayed, "That they all may be one; as thou, Father, art in me, and I in thee, that they also may be one in us: that the world may believe that thou hast sent me."[l] Jesus and His Father were so intertwined that they were inseparable. If you saw one, you saw the other. In the same way, His people are to be so intertwined with Christ and each other that it portrays the unity existing in the Godhead.

But why? What is God's purpose behind this unity? Jesus said it like this: "I in them, and thou in me . . . that the world may know . . ."[m]

---

[j] Colossians 3:17
[k] 1 Corinthians 10:31
[l] John 17:21
[m] John 17:23

God still has His eye on the lost, and He desires that His church be so united that the lives of its members attract men to Him.

What if the natural and spiritual parts of our personal lives were intertwined, creating a beautiful tapestry to the glory of God? How might this affect our businesses?

## Conclusion

In spite of all the New Testament teaching to the contrary, believers throughout the ages have still tried to separate the natural from the spiritual. They have believed in the sacredness of specific places, set up "holy" orders of men who separated themselves from ordinary life, and performed all kinds of ascetic acts designed to subdue the physical body. But God has no quarrel with our physical body. Rather, He wants to save us from our obsession with the earthly, our rebellion against authority, and our selfish desires.

God made us and understands that we are dust.[n] But He desires that we, like Jesus, live with an overriding vision of doing only those things that please Him. As we more fully comprehend the fact that the physical is to be used to glorify God, this truth will alter how we interact in daily life. It will change our worldviews. And it will change our businesses.

---

[n] Psalm 103:14

# *Analyzing Your Worldview* | 15

From the infant learning to crawl to the eighty-five-year-old man with cancer sitting down with his lawyer to make out a will, all of us have a lens through which we see the world. This worldview affects everything, even the most basic daily decisions. Our worldview affects how we set the alarm clock, how we respond to its persistent ringing, or whether or not we even use one.

Worldviews also change. We come into this world thinking about ourselves. Whether hungry, thirsty, tired, or just lacking attention, an infant's focus is universally self-centered. But as time goes by, something shifts. We become more aware of others. Even as young children, we become concerned when another child or an animal is injured. From thinking only of ourselves to becoming aware of the needs of others, our worldview naturally evolves.

Worldviews can also change in unnatural ways. Sometimes God steps in. As Saul approached Damascus, he never could have imagined the radical life transformation he was about to experience. From chasing down and persecuting Christians to preaching and convincing the Jews that Jesus was Christ, there is perhaps no more dramatic example in history of a transformed worldview. Just a few days earlier he'd seen this Jesus as the world's greatest problem. Now he saw Him as its greatest solution. Paul's interests and desires changed, and he found himself hating things that just a few days before he had loved. When God changes a man's worldview, everything about that man will change.

So how do you see the world around you? More specifically, how do you see your business world? As you interact with competitors, customers, vendors, and business associates, what kind of lens are you looking through? Have you allowed the Lord Jesus Christ to transform your business worldview? In this chapter I want to look at three potential business worldviews—three entirely different lenses through which we observe our material world. As we do this, prayerfully examine and identify the worldview that drives your business.

### The Material World: To Be Enjoyed

Larry Ellison was born in 1944 to an unwed mother living in the Bronx, New York City. His mother left him with an aunt in Chicago, and he was raised in the city's South Side.[1] Even as a small boy, Larry demonstrated a defiant spirit, clashing repeatedly with his adoptive father. But he also had a strong aptitude for math and science and was named science student of the year during his first year at the University of Illinois. During his second year of college, Larry's adoptive mother died, and he dropped out of school. He enrolled at a different college the following fall, but again dropped out after the first semester. For the next eight years Larry bounced from job to job, picking up computer skills along the way and eventually getting a job at Amdahl Corporation just as they were building the first IBM-compatible mainframe computer system.

Larry Ellison's natural abilities in science and math were quickly discovered in this inventive environment, and within just a few years Larry and a couple of colleagues founded their own software company, where Larry focused on building database management systems. Today Oracle Corporation, the business Larry started in 1977, is a leader in the software industry. In recent years Oracle has bought up many other software businesses, and Larry has become famous for risky acquisitions. The result of all this activity is that Larry Ellison, who started life in the humblest of financial settings, is one of the wealthiest men on the planet.

Larry Ellison has made a lot of money, but if you want to discern what motivates a man, you must know more than how much he makes. Discovering where that income is going will tell you much more about a man's worldview. So where has Larry's wealth gone?

Larry Ellison lives in a $200-million house in Silicon Valley, has a taste for exotic sports cars, and sails some of the most expensive yachts in the world. He is a licensed pilot and owns a retired military fighter jet.[2] It isn't difficult for observers to determine Larry Ellison's worldview. He has spent his life in a dogged attempt to squeeze as much pleasure out of life as possible. Larry Ellison's worldview is simple. The material world is something to be enjoyed. This is revealed by how he spends his income.

If someone analyzed how you spend your income, what would he conclude? Do you view the material world primarily as something to be enjoyed? Of course, few conservative Christians would want to admit this. But what would your spending habits reveal? Why are you working hard, creating business plans, and diligently attempting to expand? If you really want to analyze your worldview, look closely at where your personal resources and business profits are flowing. If your business is simply the vehicle that makes living an enjoyable life possible, then you have discovered your worldview. You view the material world as primarily something to be enjoyed.

It is possible to hold the same worldview as Larry Ellison yet live a very different life. Sometimes in our conservative churches our focus becomes narrow. I have talked with people who believe they are responsible to assist with physical needs only within their own church community or fellowship. But if all our extra resources are focused internally, and our vision goes no further than continually improving the homes, farms, and lives of those in our communities, we may just be wrapping spiritual skin around a carnal worldview centered on living an enjoyable life. Consider these words of Jesus: "When thou makest a dinner or a supper, call not thy friends, nor thy brethren, neither thy kinsmen, nor thy rich neighbors; lest they also bid thee again, and a recompense be made thee. But when thou makest a feast, call the poor, the maimed, the lame, the blind: and thou shalt be blessed; for they cannot recompense thee: for thou shalt be recompensed at the resurrection of the just."[a]

---

[a] Luke 14:12–14

A church's members should be known for helping each other. This is one of the ways the world sees that Jesus is present within that church.[b] But if we fail to reach out beyond our borders, it may be a self-centered pursuit—helping others, knowing that if I am ever in trouble they will help me. This is exactly what Jesus taught against. Are we giving only to those we know will help us if we ever face a need? Or are we, as Jesus exhorted, blessing those who have no ability to recompense? We are well able to live devout outward lives, yet be so internally focused that we miss the blessing of furthering the Kingdom of God. This can become little more than self-centered living in spiritual skin.

## The Material World: To Be Shunned

Few men have achieved fame for so strange a feat, but if you had lived in Aleppo, Syria, in the fifth century, you would have known of Simeon the Stylite.[3] As a young man, Simeon developed a zeal for Christianity. Trying to apply the Beatitudes, Simeon began to fast and abstain from human company for long periods of time. Jesus said the poor, the meek, the hungry, and the thirsty would be blessed, so Simeon shut himself in a hut, remaining there a long time without food or drink. Other times he sequestered himself in isolated places, on the sides of cliffs, or in constricted spaces. Yet no matter how hard Simeon tried to avoid people, the masses continued to find him. Crowds of pilgrims sought him out, asking for his counsel and prayers. In fact, Simeon was so inundated by visitors that he couldn't find enough time alone with God, so he finally resorted to living on a small platform on top of a pillar.

The first pillar Simeon scaled was a little more than nine feet high, but it was replaced by others, the last in the series being over fifty feet high. Simeon's goal was to separate himself from the comforts of the material world he lived in. He viewed the world as something to be shunned. Concerned people brought ladders and gave Simeon water and food to keep him from starving. But other than this occasional nourishment, he avoided all worldly pleasure. For thirty-seven years Simeon lived on top of this pillar. Reports say he never erected any protection against the elements or accepted any medical aid. He planned

---

[b] John 13:35

to remain on his post until death, and his mission was accomplished when he died on September 2, A.D. 459.[4]

Simeon inspired many other pole sitters. History tells of many who erected pillars and lived atop them in an attempt to shun the world's comforts. These men viewed the ascetic lifestyle as the best way to live out Christ's command to "love not the world."[c] As you read their accounts, it is easy to discern their worldview. They saw the material world as something to be shunned.

I know of no one today who is attempting to serve God by living on top of a post. But some of us, especially Servant Sams, tend toward the belief that the material world is bad and something to be avoided. Instead of avoiding contact with this world by erecting a pole, we may be tempted to withdraw from the battle—to find some nice place to enjoy our lives and insulate ourselves from the tremendous needs in the lives of others. Maybe a long lane in a nice rural setting allows us to retreat from the surrounding chaos and confusion.

There is nothing wrong with living in the country or trying to separate our families to some extent from an ungodly culture. Some of this is necessary if our children are going to survive. But we also need to be reminded and warned. Jesus does not want His people to be taken out of the world.[d] He intends that we be working, and there is much to be done.

Years ago we became involved in foster care. This opened our eyes to how little we had known about the struggles within a certain segment of our society. We knew some people in our county were poor, but we

[c] 1 John 2:15
[d] John 17:15

had given little thought to their lives. Being part of a strong conservative community is a wonderful thing. It helps insulate us from much of the evil in our society. But if we are not careful, it can also insulate us from needs and from the very people God is calling us to serve.

Charles Wesley wrote a hymn that begins with a solemn declaration, "A charge to keep I have," and goes on to itemize what God has called His followers to. Wesley addressed the fact that we are to glorify God, and we must seriously consider the eternal fate of our own souls. But in the second verse he shifted his gaze to the responsibility we have to others. "To serve the present age, my calling to fulfill. O, may it all my powers engage to do my Master's will." I have sung this and wondered, *Am I really demonstrating the love of Jesus to others and serving them, or am I just trying to survive? God has called us to live separate lives, but have I taken this too far? Am I interacting with the hurting enough to bless them? Is my goal to serve, or just to survive?*

At first glance there is a major difference between sitting on a pole in the fifth century and withdrawing from society today. Yet there comes a point at which our separation may be little more than sanctified laziness. Millions around the globe have great physical and spiritual needs. In our local communities many are confused, lonely, and disillusioned. Many are seeking meaning in life, and in Jesus we have the answer. It is possible, under the banner of separation, to draw back from the battle and neglect our mission. This sort of withdrawal may actually be self-serving.

> **There comes a point at which our separation may be little more than sanctified laziness.**

### The Material World: To Be Used for the Kingdom

I believe God does want us to enjoy life. I think He takes pleasure in seeing a man enjoy good food, a night's rest, or time with his family. There is also a time to come apart from the world and rest a while. As children of God, we need times of quiet contemplation, and sometimes this can best take place by separating ourselves from the surrounding chaos for a time. But it is important to understand that neither of these worldviews is complete in itself. Paul told the church at Corinth that believers "should not henceforth live unto themselves, but unto him which died for them, and rose again."[e] Our primary goal is to be actively engaged in working with God.

But what does all this have to do with my business? It means that every aspect of my life, including my business, is to become engaged in the same work God is engaged in. Paul goes on in this chapter to explain that God has an intense desire to see humanity reconciled to Him, and He has committed unto us this same ministry of reconciliation.

Our world was wonderful when first created. God said it was good. But it has been cursed due to man's fall into sin. From an eternal perspective, our material world is on a short timeline and will soon be gone. There is nothing wrong with enjoying times of rest or the blessings God has provided. God intended that we enjoy them. The Apostle Paul told Timothy that God has "given us richly all things to enjoy."[f] But before we run out, like Larry Ellison, and embrace a worldview that sees the material world as something primarily to be enjoyed, we need to read the surrounding verses in that passage. God provides wealth for a specific purpose, and Paul says it is to aid in good works and to be distributed to others.[g] It is to be shared and used in this ministry of reconciliation.

**Conclusion**

Jesus gave specific instructions on the proper use of our gifts and talents, and He isn't pleased with men who bury them or spend their lives sitting on a pole. God intends that we do more than just shun the material world. But the Bible is also clear that men will be condemned in the final judgment for not sharing and for heaping the fruits of their labors on themselves.[h] There are strong warnings throughout Jesus' teachings regarding this.

[e] 2 Corinthians 5:15
[f] 1 Timothy 6:17
[g] 1 Timothy 6:17–19
[h] James 5:1–6

> **It is extremely important for the Christian businessman to have a correct worldview—to understand not just the proper procedures of business, but the powerful purpose.**

It is extremely important for the Christian business-man to have a correct worldview—to understand not just the proper procedures of business, but the powerful purpose.

Unless we have a Biblical understanding of why we are in business, it will be difficult to apply Jesus' teachings. As we begin to comprehend God's heartbeat, we will see our daily business life as an integral part of God's work. God is not opposed to natural things; He made them. He intends that our businesses exist to further the Kingdom of God. As Paul told the church at Corinth, "We are workers together with Him."[i]

---

[i] 2 Corinthians 6:1

# PART FOUR

*Kingdom Business: An*
*Intentional Pursuit*

# A Kingdom-Focused Foundation  16

Immediately following Japan's surprise attack on Pearl Harbor in World War II, the United States searched for some dramatic response. There was a deep desire to retaliate in a way that communicated the United States' commitment and resolve to Japan, so a bold plan was devised. They would drop bombs directly on Tokyo itself! But there were some major hurdles to overcome before this could happen. There were no airfields close enough to Japan to launch an attack. So sixteen B-25s were specially modified, enabling them to take off from an aircraft carrier. Extra fuel tanks were installed to provide the aircraft with as much range as possible, and anything unnecessary for the mission was removed to decrease the weight. The tail gunner section was removed and red painted broomsticks hung out the back, replicating the missing machine guns. Heavy bombers had never been launched this way before. Yet the desire to strike back was so strong that the U.S. armed forces were willing to take risks.

Though they had overcome the challenge of getting these heavy planes into the air, they faced an even greater obstacle to their mission. The planes couldn't carry enough fuel to make a round trip even with the extra fuel tanks. So the eighty crew members knew they wouldn't be able to fly back to the carrier after their mission. They would drop their bombs on Japan and then fly toward China, hoping to find a place to land there.

It was an incredibly risky plan, and every one of the men who volunteered was well aware of the danger. Yet these men agreed to go, knowing full well their odds of survival were small. They were driven by a passion to defend their country.

On the day of the raid, things got even worse. The Japanese military had caught wind of the plan, and the U.S. carrier was forced to move farther from Japan than previously planned. This meant the bombers would not have enough fuel to make it to China. They would have to bomb Japan and then fend for themselves. Each of the men was given a chance to back out, yet none did. They bombed Tokyo and then flew as far as they could. Four of the planes crashed, eleven crews bailed out, and one crew made it to Russia. Of the eighty airmen who went, sixty-two survived the war, far more than the military had expected.[1]

This raid sent a powerful message to Japan and the rest of the world. The risk demonstrated their deep resolve to fight for their country. It is one thing to hear a man talk about loving his country or to see him hang out a flag or attend a local patriotic parade. It is entirely another to watch him crawl into a cockpit and take off, fully aware that he lacks the fuel to return.

Today we are not called to fight against a physical foe, but we are engaged in a battle. And for the Christian businessman, the fight to remain focused on the Kingdom of God is just as intense. When those men left that carrier and headed out over the Pacific Ocean, they couldn't afford to think about their own personal wellbeing. I don't think their minds were on the comfort of their seats, the temperature in the cockpit, or whether or not the flight was smooth. They weren't driven by desire for personal safety or comfort. They were driven by something much stronger—probably a mixture of patriotism, solidarity with fellow soldiers, and a desire for retaliation. A preoccupation with personal comfort would have meant death to their mission.

This is true in Christian business as well. If your business is going to be useful within the Kingdom of God, it will take sacrifice. You will need to be driven by something stronger than a self-centered pursuit of the American dream.

We looked at our tendency to separate the spiritual part of our lives from the secular, and at Jesus as the perfect example of an interwoven life. But what does that look like in the business world? How are we to dress all these lofty spiritual truths in work clothes and make our businesses a blessing to the Kingdom of God? There are bills to pay, difficult customers to work with, and deadlines to meet. How can the Kingdom of God be woven into business life?

Jesus taught that a man who builds his personal life on anything other than His teachings will fail.[a] I believe this is also true of a Kingdom-focused business. If we are going to successfully live out the commands of Jesus in our business life, we must build on the right foundation. Consider Paul's teaching to the church at Ephesus. He said, "Let him that stole steal no more: but rather let him labour, working with his hands the thing which is good, that he may have to give to him that needeth."[b] This familiar passage contains a wonderful outline for a Kingdom-focused business.

1. Absolute honesty. "Let him that stole steal no more . . ."
2. Strong work ethic. ". . . but rather let him labour, working with his hands . . ."
3. A blessing to the community. ". . . the thing that is good . . ."
4. A Kingdom-focused vision. ". . . that he may have to give to him that needeth."

**A Kingdom-Focused Foundation**
Picture for a moment building a business in the shape of a

Kingdom-Focused Vision

[a] Matthew 7:21–27
[b] Ephesians 4:28

pyramid from this outline. Starting from the ground up, we begin with a Kingdom-focused vision. Everything that happens within this business is built upon this foundation. Regardless how small the decision or activity, it will have the ultimate goal of furthering the Kingdom of Jesus Christ. No part will be exempt.

The Bible is clear that we are to provide for our own households, and God intends that we use business profit to sustain ourselves. But this passage reveals that God has more in mind than just providing for our families. He intends that we conduct our businesses with a foundational motive of helping those in need and blessing the Kingdom. So let's start by laying the foundation of a Kingdom-focused vision.

## A Blessing to the Community

Paul said that our occupations should consist of things that are good. In other words, a business built upon a Kingdom-focused foundation will be interested in more than just the profit and loss statement. It will also provide something beneficial for the community. There are many occupations that produce tremendous revenue, yet are not a blessing. Think of all the commercial ventures that, though lucrative, are damaging to the social fiber of our society. Income is not the only goal, and a Kingdom-focused business will have a goal to bless the community.

## A Strong Work Ethic

"Let him labour," Paul says, "working with his hands." I get a picture here of industry and a good work ethic. The teachings of Proverbs address this. "He that tilleth the land shall have plenty of bread."ᶜ There is nothing wrong with industry when it is built on a Kingdom-focused foundation. In fact, God expects it. Paul reiterated this thought in his letter to the church at Thessalonica when he said, "If any would not work, neither should he eat."ᵈ God desires that His people be diligent and known for a strong work ethic.

## Absolute Honesty

"Let him that stole steal no more." A Kingdom-focused business will be known for absolute honesty and ethical behavior at every level. When we tell someone we will be there, that we will finish a project on a certain date, or that the check is in the mail, they should have full confidence this is true. Many businesses advertise that they are Christian businesses. But all of this is vain, and even detrimental to the cause of the Gospel, if the business lacks basic honesty.

## The Kingdom-Focused Business

Look for a moment at this diagram and get a picture of how a business could look. If your business is truly built upon a Kingdom-focused vision, it only follows that this business will bless the community. God has always desired to bless, so why wouldn't a business that represents Him do the same? And since His Word instructs us to not be slothful in business, serving the Lord,ᵉ you would expect a strong work ethic. It would be foolish for a lazy worker to pass out tracts or witness to fellow workers. Something inside tells us this is inconsistent. And finally, honesty is a characteristic of God Himself. It is Satan who is the notorious liar. The people of God are known for truth. A businessman who is following Jesus will relentlessly pursue

Honesty

Strong Work Ethic

Blessing to Community

Kingdom-Focused Vision

ᶜ Proverbs 28:19

ᵈ 2 Thessalonians 3:10

ᵉ Romans 12:11

absolute honesty, even if the financial cost is great.[f]

**Analyzing Your Business**

Consider your business. Is it built upon a Kingdom foundation? Does every decision, regardless how small, honor God and reflect the teachings of Jesus? It is possible for our businesses to have other foundational goals. I can think of times in my life, to my own shame, when I moved off this foundation. The lure of financial gain was so great that I built on something else.

All of us, but especially Production Pauls, will face this temptation. Perhaps we have extremely difficult customers or are trying to meet important deadlines, and suddenly the money we might lose or gain seems extremely important. But when the value of the transaction becomes more valuable than the soul of the individual involved, we have slipped off the proper footing. It is time to go back and determine on which foundation we are building.

> When the value of the transaction becomes more valuable than the soul of the individual involved, we have slipped off the proper footing.

What about the products or services we provide? Are they blessing our communities? Or is it possible, in our efforts to make our businesses more profitable, that this detail has been overlooked? It seems we must continually go back and revisit why we do what we do. The world's values can easily rub off on us, and if we are going to operate a business that honors God and furthers His Kingdom, we must frequently examine our business life. A secular proverb says, "The price of freedom is eternal vigilance."[g]

**Conclusion**

When those men launched their bombers off the aircraft carrier during

---

[f] Psalm 15:4

[g] The origin of this quote is unknown. It has been attributed to Thomas Jefferson, Thomas Paine, Abraham Lincoln, and many others.

World War II, they had no way of knowing if they would be alive by nightfall. But they were committed to their mission. How committed are you to using your business for the good of the Kingdom of God? Are you willing, like those courageous pilots, to risk everything? Those pilots were fighting a physical battle with no guarantees. But our battle is far different, and we have promises from our Commander. He has not assured us of financial success, but He has promised that He will be with us and meet our needs. Jesus Himself said it like this: "Seek ye first the kingdom of God, and his righteousness; and all these things shall be added unto you."[h]

---

[h] Matthew 6:33

# *You're Being Watched!* | 17

Beginning operations on August 3, 1972, Hobby Lobby started out with only 300 square feet of retail space. In the following thirty years the corporation experienced exponential growth, and by 2014 they had 572 stores across America averaging 55,000 square feet per store.[1] But Hobby Lobby isn't famous primarily for its growth. Other companies have grown much faster. Rather, Hobby Lobby frequently finds itself in the news due to its unabashed stand on religion. "We're Christians," Hobby Lobby president Steve Green boldly proclaims, "and we run our business on Christian principles."[2]

From the beginning, the company claims, they have honored the Lord by operating in a manner consistent with Biblical principles. They declare their intention to share profits with their employees and invest in local communities where they operate.

Though the decision has been costly, they close all their stores every Sunday. "We believe that it is by God's grace and provision that Hobby Lobby has endured," their website proclaims. "God has been faithful in the past, and we trust Him for our future."[3]

This public declaration of faith, coupled with their recent highly publicized healthcare battle in the Supreme Court, has brought the company tremendous publicity. It has also brought intense scrutiny and criticism. "Stop Calling Hobby Lobby a Christian Business," one headline read. "Turn over just about any trinket in a Hobby Lobby store and you'll find a gold oval stamped with 'Made in China,' a country that is one of the worst offenders of human dignity, unborn infant life, and economic justice anywhere in the world," the article went on to say. The author alleges that Hobby Lobby is being hypocritical. "If Hobby Lobby was concerned with religious freedoms—not just those of conservative American Christians—it would quit doing business in China."

Other reporters have jumped on this issue as well, some of them even professing Christians. "What would Jesus do?" asks Leslie Marshall, a professing believer with *U.S. News and World Report* who feels the company is inconsistent. "He would remind Hobby Lobby that he that is without sin among you, let him cast the first stone. Hobby Lobby should put its stones down. And America should put down its "Made in China" products."[4]

Whatever you think about a company that professes to operate on Christian principles while importing billions of dollars in merchandise each year from China, one thing is clear. If you are going to proclaim that your enterprise is a Christian business, you are going to be watched closely.

### Christian Businesses Are Being Watched

The media and those looking on have every right to examine our claims. If we say our businesses are Christian, then we shouldn't be afraid to have our claims tested. So how would your business hold up under close examination? In the last chapter we looked at the importance of having a Kingdom-focused foundation and of making daily business choices that flow out of this foundational desire to glorify God. In this chapter I want to examine how we are doing. I am not so worried about whether CNN is impressed with our scorecard. But I am concerned about what the Lord would have to say.

One of the burdens I have, and the driving impetus in writing this book, is that our conservative churches are having difficulty grasping the great potential business has within the Kingdom of God. We understand that a business should be honest, maintain a good reputation, and honor the Lord's Day. But do we understand why God has called us to interact in the business world? I have met many young people who seem to believe the Kingdom of God would grow faster if they didn't have to go to work anymore—if their natural needs were met from some other source so they could devote all their waking hours to "full-time ministry." But what if God intends for your business to be the vehicle through which others come to see Jesus? What if, rather than just a means to fund ministries, business became a ministry in itself?

> What if, rather than just a means to fund ministries, business became a ministry in itself?

In the Sermon on the Mount Jesus gave instruction regarding how our daily lives should impact those who are watching. He said, "Let your light so shine before men, that they may see your good works, and glorify your Father which is in heaven."[a] Jesus wasn't just telling us to make sure our mission programs have a positive impact on others. He was telling us that every part of our lives should point to the Father. And since a large part of the average believer's life will be lived out in the marketplace, shouldn't we consider how to accomplish this?

### How Are We Doing?

Listening to business owners in our conservative churches share their struggles and dreams, and observing how they conduct their businesses, I believe there are some things we are doing right. In the last chapter we used Paul's instruction to the church at Ephesus as an outline

---

[a] Matthew 5:16

for Christian business. We looked at the importance of honesty, having a good work ethic, being a blessing in our communities, and building upon a Kingdom-focused foundation. Now let's look at how we are doing in these four areas. I understand that there are exceptions to the overall observations I am going to share. But I think it is important for us to occasionally back up and look at what the world might be seeing, because they are watching.

**Honesty**

As I look at these four basic components, the one that stands out most is honesty. Ask almost anyone, and they will tell you that conservative Christian businesses are known for honesty and integrity. It is a strong point.

In 2010, business writer Erik Wesner set out to explain why the Amish are succeeding in business. While some studies have shown that 65 percent of North American small businesses fail during the first seven years, the failure rate of Amish startups was less than 5 percent.[5] How can this be? How can a segment of society that remains off the power grid, still uses horses for transportation, and shuns technology even compete in today's marketplace? Beyond that, how can 95 percent of new business startups succeed while working within these stringent parameters? Erik uncovered many factors, but one of the primary reasons for success was the Amish insistence on quality and honesty in business. "Quality is a running narrative in Amish business circles,"[6] he stated in his book.

In 2009, a *New York Times* article regarding the Amish said, "Despite a lack of even a high school education (the Amish leave school after the eighth grade), hundreds of Amish entrepreneurs have built profitable businesses based on the Amish values of high quality, integrity, and hard work."[7] The Amish have become famous for integrity and honesty. When you purchase an "Amish pie," you expect to get a good one. In fact, the word *Amish* has become so synonymous with honesty and reliability that we see it used in a variety of marketing schemes. While driving across the country several years ago, I saw a sign advertising an "Amish Truck Stop." I have even seen ads attempting to market "Amish Computer Software." A reputation for honesty is worth having and guarding.

## Work Ethic

The second area we are doing well in is having a good work ethic. Some have shared concerns that our youth today are not as willing to work as previous generations have been. I am sure we have been affected by American culture in this area, but overall this is still a strong point of the Plain People. Many customers are willing to wait for work crews from these conservative communities, knowing they will receive quality labor and workmanship. This is good, and care needs to be taken to not lose our witness in this area.

## Blessing the Community

We looked at the importance of intentionally producing products and providing services that bless our communities. Regretfully, I have to say this one is a little sketchy. While there are good examples of businesses that purposefully try to do this, for many it seems this virtue is sacrificed on the altar of increased earnings. Recently there have been several news articles highlighting Plain People involved in get-rich-quick schemes. Millions of dollars have been invested in risky schemes to develop resorts in Florida, while others have been guilty of chasing high investment returns and losing money that had been entrusted to them. At a recent meeting in a conservative community, I was amazed at the level of affluence where the meeting was held. Everything from the huge home to the elaborate landscaping spoke of wealth. The owner belonged to a very conservative group, so I asked one of the local people where this man had made his money. Evidently the owner had been an early investor in a multi-level marketing scheme, and his initial investment had provided an excellent return.

Unfortunately, many of our conservative communities are known for chasing get-rich-quick schemes, and it isn't uncommon to find conservative people involved in multi-level marketing programs. These programs are famous for being driven by greed with little regard for the consumer.

If we are called to demonstrate the Gospel of Jesus through our interaction in the marketplace, can this be accomplished by being involved in these types of activities? We claim to follow a Man who taught that "a man's life consisteth not in

> ## Can we effectively persuade others to take a closer look at the Kingdom of God when we esteem income and wealth just as highly as they do?

the abundance of the things which he possesseth."[b] But can we effectively persuade others to take a closer look at the Kingdom of God when we esteem income and wealth just as highly as they do?

The homes I worked on when I did residential construction were large and elaborate, and sometimes I wondered if my work was actually blessing our community. Is it right to build and sell things I wouldn't feel good about owning myself? Would Jesus build huge homes He wouldn't feel comfortable living in? How much responsibility do we bear for what others ask us to do or for the way they use what we produce? While it may not be possible to draw definitive lines for every situation, I wonder if there is a difference between providing a product or service upon request and encouraging unbiblical consumption.

This can be a very fine line, but I know I have crossed it. Due to my building experience, I could picture ways a room could be "dressed up" and would share suggestions that encouraged ostentatious decisions. The customers appreciated it, and I could argue that it was what they were paying me to do. But sometimes I returned home wondering. Had I encouraged others to continue down a path of materialistic madness? Was I living in hypocrisy, on the one hand professing to be a follower of the Man who scorned what was highly esteemed, but on the other helping customers waste resources to impress their friends?

These are difficult issues, but in our covetous culture we need to prayerfully consider them. If Jesus were a business owner today, I believe He would be interested in producing an income. But more than that, I think He would have a goal of producing products or providing

---

[b] Luke 12:15

services that would bless His community.

**A Kingdom-Focused Foundation**

Every business is built upon some foundation. Something motivates the decisions each day. Some make every decision based solely on profit. For others it may be on reputation. Businessmen experience strong peer pressure, and the desire to impress others can drive decisions. Those of us who have grown up in close communities where we are used to meeting others' expectations in dress and other areas can be especially gullible to this.

But a Kingdom-driven business will operate differently. Each decision will be based not on potential profit or standing among other businessmen, but on furthering the Kingdom of God. We can do better in this area. People see us as having good morals, building things of good quality, and demonstrating a good work ethic. But there are many self-centered reasons that can motivate us to be honest, to use quality in production, and to be diligent. How many of us are willing to lose money to demonstrate Christianity? We need to hear more stories of believers who have gone beyond what is expected in business, even though they gained nothing materially.

It seems the primary goal for too many is to produce adequate funding to enjoy an affluent lifestyle, and then, as an afterthought, to share with those in need. Instead of being the underlying, foundational motivation of the business, as Paul encouraged the church at Ephesus,[c] giving becomes secondary. The result is a public perception that these quaint people are driven by the same love of money that drives the rest of the business world.

**Conclusion**

I have shared my observations of our conservative Christian businesses. Perhaps yours have been different. But if what I have shared has some truth in it, we should be alarmed, because there's a fundamental problem. Our strong point, or foundation, should be a Kingdom-focused vision, and virtues like honesty and a good work ethic should

---

[c] Ephesians 4:28

flow from this. But my observation has been that honesty is our strong
point, followed closely by a good work ethic, and our Kingdom vision
is lacking. Prayerfully consider the diagrams below. Which best represents your business?

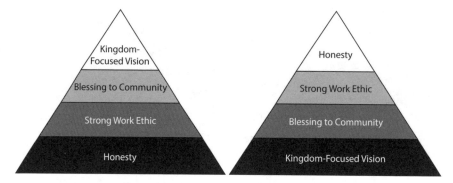

# *What If . . . ?*  |  18

Born in 1494, William Tyndale looked around at the religious culture he lived in with dismay. People had a desire to follow God, but there was little firsthand knowledge about what the Bible actually taught. How could people be expected to live righteous lives when the church leaders themselves showed little interest in holiness and a good English Bible was unavailable? Tyndale himself was a highly educated man. Fluent in several languages, including Greek and Hebrew, he could read the Word of God for himself. But for the common man in England, owning and reading a Bible wasn't conceivable. There had been previous attempts to translate parts of the Bible into English, but the church had gone to great lengths to keep these copies from the common people. Consequently, no affordable English version was available.

Tyndale voiced his concern, yet received little support from his well-educated peers. "It would be wrong to translate God's holy Word into English," one religious scholar reportedly told him. "Only a language like Latin or Greek is able to fully convey God's truth. English is a vulgar language—fine for plowmen and shopkeepers, but hardly suitable for the Bible."[1]

In spite of strong pressure from the religious establishment of the day, Tyndale couldn't forget the vision. He dreamed of an England where everyone, even the plowman, could have access to a Bible written in his mother tongue—English. William Tyndale risked his life to bring this dream to reality. Moving out of the country for security reasons, he set about translating the New Testament into common English, and by 1526, copies of Tyndale's Bible began flowing into England. Purposely made small, these Bibles were smuggled inside bales of cotton and containers of wheat being shipped into England. As the Bibles poured into the country, people eagerly purchased them. They sat up all night reading these books or hearing them read. Many people were thrown into prison just for being caught with this "dangerous" and illegal book, and thousands were martyred.

Tyndale's Bible was like a flame thrown into the dry tinder of human hearts in England, and the country would never be the same. Many came to know the Lord and were changed simply because one man risked his life to bring them the Word of God. But why did William Tyndale take this great risk? What caused him to leave all that he had and head down this hazardous path?

## What If . . . ?

William Tyndale looked at the ignorance, the resulting ungodliness, and the way the poor were financially oppressed by the priests. He saw the lies promoted by the church hierarchy, the grave misunderstandings people held about God Himself, and he wondered . . . *What if these people could read the Bible for themselves? What if there was a Bible so inexpensive and easy to read that even the common plowman could read it to his family in the evenings?*

William Tyndale dared to ask, "What if . . . ?" All through history God has longed for men and women who are willing to ask this question.

## God's Plan for Israel

Think back to God's dealings with the children of Israel. Throughout most of the Old Testament God worked (and struggled) with the Israelites. They were a rebellious bunch, and we follow God's many merciful, creative efforts to persuade them to willingly follow Him. But why did God go to all this trouble? There may be several good answers to this question, but there is one truth we dare not ignore. God wanted to demonstrate His power to all the nations, and He chose Israel as the stage for His demonstration. He wanted other nations to look at Israel's laws, the order of their assemblies, and at how God delivered them when they found themselves in trouble. And He wanted these nations to respond by asking, "What if . . . ?"

*What if things worked as beautifully in our country as they do in Israel? What if we went out to battle and the opposing army's city walls fell down the way Jericho's did? What if we had a God who could attack our enemies with hailstones? What if the God they serve was our God? What if the entire world served this God of Israel? What an amazing world that would be! What if . . . ?*

Notice the words of the Psalmist as he explains God's intent: "God be merciful unto us, and bless us; and cause his face to shine upon us;" What was the purpose behind this request? "That thy way may be known upon earth, thy saving health among all nations."[a] This is just one verse of many that share an important and powerful message. God wasn't blessing Israel so they could all have nice lives and enjoy themselves. It wasn't about them at all. He intended for that nation to demonstrate what the whole world could be like if everyone followed God.

When the Queen of Sheba visited King Solomon, God was glorified. She looked around at the beauty of Solomon's kingdom and at the way everything worked so smoothly. She even took notice of the happiness of his servants. She was so amazed that the Bible says "there was no more spirit in her."[b] She had heard wonderful things about this kingdom, which is why she had visited. But the reality of the experience was better than she had anticipated.

She left there telling others that, in spite of all she had heard before, "the half was not told me."[c] Can't you imagine her thoughts as she returned to her own country? She had just witnessed the result of allegiance and obedience to Almighty God! She had seen a public demonstration of what happens when a nation wholeheartedly serves the God of the universe! I can see her traveling home thinking, *What could my nation become if we followed God?* And perhaps a couple of miles down the road, *What if the whole world followed this God? What would that be like?*

This is God's ultimate desire for His church. While God intends that we find refreshment as we gather for worship, the church is to be much more than just a place to make us feel good. It is to be a public

---

[a] Psalm 67:1, 2
[b] 1 Kings 10:5
[c] 1 Kings 10:7

> "The church is to be a public corporate demonstration of what the entire world could be like if everyone followed Jesus."

corporate demonstration of what the entire world could be like if everyone followed Jesus. Seekers should look over the walls of our churches and say, "Look how they love each other! Notice how they take care of those who have struggles and how they provide for the weak among them! They have something we don't have. What if our entire nation worked so beautifully? What if their God were my God? What if . . . ?"

### God's Business Plan

Businessmen give thought to business goals and long-term vision. They go to seminars and learn the differences between mission statements and vision statements. They develop marketing strategies and discuss the importance of company core values. But have you ever considered the possibility that God might have a business plan in mind as well, a purpose and goal for your business beyond just generating enough income for you and your family to live in comfort? I want to suggest that God does have a goal and vision for your business, and it's much grander than just producing income. The Christian business, like the church, is to be a public demonstration that shows what the world of commerce could be like if every businessman followed Jesus. People who walk out the doors of your establishment should be thinking, *What if every business operated like that?*

### A Public Demonstration

George owned a family-operated carpet and upholstery cleaning business. This small enterprise provided a good income for his family and gave George many opportunities to meet and interact with customers in his community. But George had a deep desire to do more than just make an income. He viewed his business as a vehicle for the Kingdom of God and constantly looked for openings to speak to individuals about their need for a Saviour. One day George was cleaning carpet in an upscale home, and while moving a piece of very expensive furniture, he accidently scratched it. The owner wasn't home and the damage was so slight there was a slim chance anyone would notice it.

George wasn't a connoisseur of fine furniture, yet he was well aware that this chair wasn't something you would find in the local furniture store. And this customer was a well-known lawyer. He could imagine the potential repercussions arising from this little incident. But George also knew that, as a follower of Jesus Christ, there was only one correct course of action. So he waited till the lawyer returned home and then confessed what had happened. George showed him the scratch, told how it happened, and offered to pay for the damage.

The lawyer listened to George's explanation and confession, examined the chair, and then replied thoughtfully. He said the chair had been imported from Egypt, and any kind of repair would be extremely expensive—much more expensive than George had even imagined. But he went on to say, "The chair is valuable to me, but of even greater importance is the fact that you came and told me. I would not have noticed the damage for a long time, if ever. And I don't think there is another person in our entire community who would have come and told me. There is no way I could ask you to pay for the damage."

That lawyer works every day with people trying to protect themselves and limit their liability. Against this backdrop, George's honest willingness to accept blame, even though he could have easily hidden the evidence, was amazing. That lawyer shared this story when he returned to work, and several years later the impact of that little encounter was still rippling through that community.

The dog-eat-dog business environment we work in provides an awesome backdrop for a Kingdom-focused business to shine. Business owners are expected to look out for number one, so opportunities to demonstrate something different are endless. That lawyer must have headed back to his office asking himself, *What if every businessman out there was like that carpet cleaner? What if the entire world operated like that? What if . . . ?*

## What About Your Business?

When people finish interacting with you on a business level, what questions are going through their minds? Do they see you living one way in church and a completely different way in your business? Do they perceive you to be serious about following Jesus and living separate from the world at home and at church, but willing to blend in with the corporate world? Does this raise questions in the minds of those who deal with you? Do they walk away from business transactions pondering the strange dichotomy between your church and business life? Or do they walk away thinking, *Wow! What would the world of commerce be like if everyone operated their business like that?*

## Conclusion

Too often we fail to achieve God's best in business because of earthbound goals. We become accustomed to operating styles primarily patterned after unbelieving professionals and advisers. But God is constantly looking for men who, like William Tyndale, are willing to imagine something greater, men who choose to ignore what is normal and envision something far grander. I believe this is where God is calling us as Christian businessmen today. Don't get bogged down by comparing your business with other businesses. Allow God to call you to a higher vision.

Imagine your customers receiving a marketplace experience unlike anything they have ever known. Envision the impact your business could have on the Kingdom of God, not just in its ability to produce income to be sent to missions on the other side of the globe, but to present Christ in your daily interactions at home. We need enterprises built firmly upon a Kingdom-focused foundation—businesses that cause people to pause mid-step and say, "Wow, imagine what our world would be like if everyone followed Jesus! What if . . . ?"

# "The Dollar Isn't King Here!" 19

Larry Burkett once told about the owner of a large manufacturing company who suddenly lost his plant manager.[1] The manager met him at the door one morning and abruptly announced he was quitting. The owner was perplexed. For five years he had been grooming this plant manager to become president of the company. He asked the manager his reasons for leaving, but the manager refused to discuss it. The owner asked if he would at least stay long enough to train someone to take his place, but the manager responded angrily and refused. The owner was still confused, but since the manager had been a good friend, he held a going-away party, thanked him for his faithfulness, and gave him a substantial severance bonus.

Several months later the former manager's reasons for leaving became evident when he opened his own company and copied his former boss's best-selling product. During the next few years the new business grew and became a fierce competitor of the first company. But nine years later something happened. The new business had some design problems with one of its products and faced several lawsuits.

The owner of the original business was a Christian and had forgiven his former manager years before. When he heard of his competitor's difficulty, he felt God's call to reach out, so he bought one of the defective products that caused the lawsuits and asked his engineers to find a solution to the problem. They fixed the problem and tested the improvements they had made. The owner called his former manager and shared the solution his engineers had discovered.

What are your thoughts as you read a story like this? Does this account seem like occupational suicide? Does it strike you as good way to go broke? Or is there something in this factory owner's response that speaks to you of genuine Christianity? Your reaction may also help you answer another question:

## Who Is King of Your Business?

You don't need to be very perceptive to understand that the dollar is king in our secular business world. Consequently, every business decision is based on what will produce the greatest return. Seminars teach the importance of treating the customer right—so the customer will buy more. A multitude of books advise treating employees fairly and showing appreciation for their hard work—so they will work even harder. We are taught to exceed the expectations of our customers— so they will return and consume even more.

Indeed, it is hard to find business advice out there that doesn't have its roots, almost exclusively, in increased profit. Now, for any business to be viable in the long-term it must be profitable, and there is nothing wrong with making customers happy so they will return, or treating employees well so they will produce. But shouldn't the follower of Jesus be interested in much more than this? Would Jesus' only interest be in the bottom line of the profit and loss statement?

If you are perplexed by the way the owner of the manufacturing company responded to his former employee, it may be because you have become accustomed to the dollar sitting on the throne in business. This happens so subtly. Making a profit can be difficult. In the daily battle for profitability, we can forget the bigger picture, and the dollar slips back onto the throne. But we must remember that when this happens, the Lord Jesus moves off. They cannot share the throne. "No man can serve two masters: for either he will hate the one, and love the other; or else he will hold to the one, and despise the other. Ye cannot serve God and mammon."[a]

Both are masters, capable of ruling. Your business can be ruled by the dollar, or it can be ruled by God, but Jesus is clear: they can't both be on the throne at the same time. It is important to carefully analyze which

---

[a] Matthew 6:24

is reigning. The wise man said a long time ago, "He that loveth silver shall not be satisfied with silver; nor he that loveth abundance with increase."[b] If the dollar is ruling your business, you will find your business engaged in an unending quest for increased financial gains. Each year is compared to the last, and the goal is to produce more profit than the previous year. A good year is when profit exceeds the year before, and a bad year is when it doesn't. Most of us are familiar with this logic. But what would a business look like with God on the throne?

## People versus Profit

Which is more important to God, people or profit? That is easy to answer on Sunday morning, isn't it? Of course people are more important. Jesus clearly compared the value of financial profit and the soul of a man when He said, "For what shall it profit a man, if he shall gain the whole world, and lose his own soul? Or what shall a man give in exchange for his soul?"[c] Jesus is saying there is really no comparison; the soul of one man outweighs all of the world's profit. This means that when you need to decide (and you will) between increased income and the souls of men, people will be more valuable than financial profit.

In my survey of business owners, one of the questions I asked was, "What service do you provide to your community that does nothing to increase profit?" Some had given this little thought, but I was encouraged by a few of the responses. An owner of a large sawmill shared how they dispose of their sawdust. They produce about a semi-truckload each day, and it would be much easier, he told me, to have a company come and pick it up. But instead, they have chosen to let local people pick it up for their own use at home. "It gets to be a bit of a hassle, but we feel it is a service we can provide to benefit our local community." The people receiving the sawdust are not customers, so there is no advantage to the company. But this is a small way they are choosing to focus on people instead of just profit.

Another shared how their company provides free monthly teaching

---

[b] Ecclesiastes 5:10
[c] Mark 8:36, 37

seminars to employees. These seminars are not mandatory, but the men are paid for their time, and most participate.

Several of the business owners I interviewed use their place of business to promote Biblical literature both for their clients and employees. Some place tracts on their office counters for customers, and others give their employees character-building books. One owner who has obviously put a lot of energy and focus into mentoring his men told me that a good year is when he has seen the Kingdom advancing in the hearts of his employees, even if sales were flat.

Calvin owns a large business and wants his men to learn to see past themselves. He started a fund, controlled by his employees and designed to bless people in their community. Employees can opt to have funds withdrawn from their paychecks and deposited into this fund, and the company will match their donations. Once a month the participating employees meet and discuss needs they are aware of. It might be a single mother with a large hospital bill, or an older person in need of financial help. Occasionally they receive notes from recipients who have been blessed by their help, and this encourages the men to keep sharing and looking for needs in their community.

These are just a few ways businessmen are putting people and their spiritual needs over profit. There are many more ways to use our businesses to bless others, and we understand that this is important. So why do we have difficulty maintaining this perspective? Part of the reason our businesses tend to drift away from an eternal to a secular perspective is due to where we go for advice.

## Syrian Success
Reading through parts of the Old Testament can be a little depressing. In spite of all that God had done for Israel, king after king worshiped Baal or some other god, and so few were faithful. But a small number were, and King Asa was one of these. Yet toward the end of his life he made a mistake. Another king came up against him, and Asa got scared. Rather than turning to God, Asa sent silver and gold to the king of Syria, asking for help. The Syrian king accepted his payment, rallied his troops, and helped Asa defend himself against the opposing army.

And it was a success! It cost Asa some silver and gold, but he found that calling on the Syrians when he was in trouble really worked. But what did God think about this?

The Bible says God wasn't happy about Asa's decision. God sent the prophet Hanani to Asa to voice His displeasure. Hanani said Asa had lost a tremendous blessing because he had relied on the king of Syria and not on the Lord. Though Asa got what he desired, God wasn't pleased. He wanted Asa to desire God's blessing and look to Him for counsel.

There is a lesson here for business owners as well.

### Business Coaches and Consultants

In the last ten years, there has been a surge in business coaches. According to a study conducted in 2007, $2.4 billion were spent on business coaches in the United States, with the coaching market growing at about 18 percent per year.[2] Why?

Some call on outside help because their businesses are experiencing difficulty. Others may be tempted because of peer pressure. However, I believe most are just looking for advice that will make their businesses more productive, efficient, and profitable. They are looking for new techniques or different perspectives that could enhance their businesses.

As I said earlier, business owners need to pursue profitability. But if we are going to ensure that God, rather than mammon, is sitting on the throne of our businesses, we need to be careful where we go for advice. It will be difficult to keep Jesus on the throne if your business coach views profit as the ultimate goal. King Asa went to the King of Syria when he found himself in difficulty, and even though it temporarily blessed his earthly kingdom, the net result wasn't good. God wanted Asa to rely on Him, not the secular Syrians. As the prophet finished rebuking Asa, he said, "For the eyes of the Lord run to and fro throughout the whole earth, to shew himself strong in the behalf of them whose heart is perfect toward him."[d]

There may be times to seek out secular sources for business advice. Many of us have learned from books, seminars, and even consultants who have a different basis for their decisions. But we must understand

[d] 2 Chronicles 16:9

145

that when we get frequent business advice from those who are not serious about pursuing the Kingdom of God, it will be difficult to apply their teaching without compromising Biblical principles. Paul asked the church at Corinth, "What fellowship hath righteousness with unrighteousness? And what communion hath light with darkness?"[e]

Think about these questions as you consider hiring someone to provide advice and direction. If your goal is to live for the Lord Jesus and you want your business to be a public demonstration of what the world of commerce could be like if everyone were a believer, how much advice do you want from the unbelieving world? Can you really afford to mix light with darkness? Do you really want your "Christian" business to emit a confusing swirl of gray to those who interact with it?

## Conclusion

The owner of the manufacturing company who helped his former employee in a time of crisis did so because his business was based on something other than profit. He felt God was calling him to reach out to this competitor, and the reason he heard the call was because he was listening. He was well aware that helping his competitor become more profitable and competitive was not a good way to increase his own bottom line. The reason this story is so compelling is because it's so rare to see something besides profitability on the throne.

What about your business? Is the dollar still firmly seated on the throne? Or has your pursuit of personal sanctification overflowed into your business? It is easy to drift into a business mode that, though a little more honest, looks much like the corporate world. It is possible, when considering this issue of lordship, to soothe our consciences by committing to give more of our profits away. But make no mistake: it is one thing to give God a percentage of the profits from your business, but entirely another to give Him the throne!

---

[e] 2 Corinthians 6:14

# *Obstacles or Opportunities?* 20

In the last chapter we looked at a business owner whose best employee became his greatest competitor. I don't know what problems you've faced in your business life, but I think you would agree that watching your plant manager walk out the door and then start his own company in direct competition could create anxiety. Stories like this don't remain secret long, and those who are close to the situation can't help but be affected. Business obstacles have the potential to provide a glimpse of the Kingdom that many may not have seen before.

We tend to avoid obstacles any way we can. But in this chapter we want to look at how to turn these obstacles into priceless opportunities. The Apostle Paul was no stranger to obstacles. He had been commissioned to carry the light of the Gospel to a dark world, and He did so with passion. But much of the world was still waiting to hear the message, and Paul was sitting in prison. Now that is a major obstacle! But notice his focus as he wrote to the church at Philippi: "But I would ye should understand, brethren, that the things which happened unto me have fallen out rather unto the furtherance of the gospel."[a] Paul goes on to say that many other brothers had been inspired by his willingness to suffer for Christ. In fact, seeing how Paul was handling this obstacle stimulated other brothers in the church to more confidence and boldness. Paul didn't view his prison time as a setback to his mission. Rather, he saw God transforming this obstacle into an opportunity.

---

[a] Philippians 1:12

### The Difficult Customer

While I was in the residential construction business with my brother years ago, a lady called. Her house was partially complete, and she was looking for a contractor to finish the project. We had already heard stories about this owner, and the project had gained a reputation at the local lumberyard. The owner was known to be extremely difficult, and two contractors had already been fired for not doing a good enough job. But we needed work, so we went to meet the owner and look at the house.

It didn't take long to realize that the stories about this lady were true. She was extremely particular, continually finding things wrong with everyone, including her husband. She let us know she didn't like children, told us all the problems she had experienced with previous contractors, and shared a list of grievances against her next-door neighbor. The only living thing she seemed to get along with was her dog.

We left the meeting and discussed what to do. We needed the work, but there was no question—this one would be a challenge!

We took the job, knowing we would need to pour a lot of energy into making this lady happy. As we expected, the project was difficult from the beginning, and there were a few times I wasn't sure we would make it. Perhaps the owners knew they would have difficulty finding anyone else if they fired a third contractor. When we finally finished the house, the lady was pleased, and I thought we had made a friend.

Several years later my brother received a phone call. Another lady needed a contractor and asked if we would take on her project. She mentioned that she knew the previous difficult customer, and that this former client had given us a good recommendation. This potential client finished by saying, "And if you can make *her* happy, you can make anyone happy!"

We didn't begin that original project expecting her to advertise among her friends. Actually, we were shocked to find she even had friends! But that project, which looked like nothing but hassle at the time, turned out to be a great learning experience.

The difficult customer provides a unique opportunity to model the character of Christ, and in some cases offers the side benefit of public advertisement. Rather than being an obstacle, these customers provide opportunities.

**Irreparable Problems**

Sometimes we find ourselves in situations where the problem can't be fixed—when mistakes have been made and there is no way to give the customer what he wants or maybe even deserves. Reuben operated a small tree-trimming business. He met a customer at her home and discussed some tree work she was considering. She wasn't sure about some details and said she would call Reuben later after she had discussed it with her husband. That evening she contacted Reuben and said they wanted to remove the ash tree in front of the house.

"Are you sure you want to remove the ash?" Reuben asked. "That's a nice tree. It's growing well, and I would leave it there."

"No, my husband and I have talked about it, and we want the ash tree removed," she insisted.

Reuben continued trying to convince her to leave the ash, but she wouldn't listen, so the next day Reuben went to her home while she was

at work and cut down the ash tree. Hardly had he returned home when the woman called, extremely upset. "You cut down the wrong tree!" she screamed over the phone. "This makes me so angry! When my husband gets home, he will be furious!"

Reuben hurried back to the site and tried to make sense of the situation. After getting her calmed down enough to discuss the issue, he discovered she had wanted the aspen removed, not the ash. She had simply confused the names and asked him to remove the wrong tree. Reuben now wished he had asked the woman to flag the tree she wanted removed, but it was too late. The tree had been cut down and sent through the chipper.

Some things in business can be repaired or remedied, though it might be costly. But you can't put a full-grown ash tree back in a front yard. So what should Reuben have done? He could have argued that the woman had told him to cut down the ash tree. He could have reminded her of his efforts to convince her to not have it cut down. Some might say the best business decision here would have been to forget it, not charge anything (since he probably wouldn't get paid anyway), and move on to the next job.

But as sick as Reuben was about the situation, he had a desire to redeem it. He wanted to give this woman a different view of Kingdom business, so he told her he would do whatever it took to make her happy. Reuben took full responsibility for the misunderstanding, offered to plant a new ash tree at no charge, and said he would do whatever else she wanted in an attempt to restore their relationship.

At first the woman was not to be pacified. Wrong had been done, and she wanted her tree back. But when Reuben returned the next Saturday to plant a new ash tree, she began to soften. He did other pruning work for her around the house, and the end of the story is that Reuben gained a friend. She brought iced tea out, and when Reuben said he liked it, she gave him her recipe to take home to his wife. This woman later asked him to do more work for her and told her friends.

Some problems are irreparable. You can't get a tree back out of the chipper truck and rebuild it. But situations that can't be restored can still be redeemed.

**The Power of Pleased Customers**

These difficult situations also have great potential for advertisement. Sam Walton discovered this concept years ago and pounded it into his associates. He was so enamored by the marketing potential in difficult customers that he placed a glass showcase in the lobby of their corporate office. In this four-sided glass case he proudly displayed items that had been returned to Walmart for a refund along with a note explaining the circumstance. These were ridiculous refund requests, situations in which Walmart was under no obligation to provide a refund. Yet they did.

One of these items was a big round thermometer, so old the glass front was yellow. The numbers were so faded you could hardly read them. The customer returned it saying it would no longer keep accurate temperatures. Another item was a tennis racket someone had obviously smashed into the ground. A customer had returned it saying it would no longer serve tennis balls properly. Yet another item on display was a rusted out thermos bottle a customer had returned to Walmart, saying it would no longer keep items hot. The manufacturer had discontinued this model of thermos five years before the first Walmart store opened.[1]

Yet all of these customers had received full refunds. Even though they had no receipt and were obviously taking advantage of Walmart, they all received cash. Instead of being embarrassed about being taken advantage of, Sam Walton put these items on display in an effort to impart a lesson to his employees. He knew these customers, as unethical as they might be, would go tell all their friends how easy it is to take advantage of Walmart's hassle-free return policy. This news over time would develop into a reputation. The resulting advertisement for the company would be invaluable—far greater than the financial loss. Sam's motives were purely monetary, but he was capitalizing on this basic truth: pleased customers, especially difficult ones, can provide tremendous advertisement.

### Jesus Was There First

Sam Walton's teachings were considered radical by many, and few large retail stores have taken customer service to such an extreme. But is this principle of making sure every customer is satisfied really a new concept? My mind goes to some familiar words of Jesus. "All things whatsoever ye would that men should do to you, do ye even so to them."[b] In other words, try to see each human interaction from the other person's

---

[b] Matthew 7:12

point of view. This is commonly referred to as the Golden Rule. While men like Sam Walton have used this technique solely to increase profit, every follower of Jesus should apply the Golden Rule, not just to help his business, but to demonstrate to a lost world the beauty of the Kingdom of God. In every business transaction, our goal should be to bless the other person and exhibit the character of Kingdom Christianity. When a man has this desire, obstacles will suddenly become opportunities.

How are you doing in your business? Do you have a goal that everyone you do business with gains from the transaction, not just to eventually increase sales, but because you care about the other person? Or are you so busy getting the best deal or making the sale that the other person's needs get lost in the process?

### A Great Opportunity?

Recently I heard about a man who was looking for a particular tool. It cost around $500 new, but that was more than he wanted to spend. He started watching the classified ads and garage sales for a used one, and he decided he wouldn't pay more than $300. One day he stopped at a yard sale, and there on a table was the exact tool he had been looking for. It had hardly been used, and the price tag said $35. What a wonderful opportunity! The woman was selling tools after her husband's death, and she obviously had no idea how much this tool was worth.

This man had to make a decision. Should he just pay what she was asking? After all, both would walk away from the transaction feeling good. Or should he pay her what the tool was really worth? This man was a follower of Jesus, so he told her this tool was exactly what he had been looking for and that he was willing to pay $300 for it. What caused the man to reveal the true value of the tool? It was an honest desire for mutual blessing in the transaction. As you can imagine, this shocked widow didn't keep this story to herself.

### Mutual Blessing in Every Transaction

We talk a lot about business opportunities. But is a good deal really an opportunity for a follower of Jesus when he is the only one blessed? Do you think Jesus could have walked off that widow's property feeling good about paying her $35 for a tool worth $300? Can you imagine

Jesus bragging to His friends about this good deal? I don't think so. Stories like this should be the norm. Our Christian communities should be known not just for making quality products, always telling the truth, and living quaint lives, but also for making sure everyone gains in every transaction.

## Conclusion

When you think of business opportunity, what comes to your mind? Could the difficult customer you are dealing with be an opportunity in disguise? I believe God sends difficult situations into our businesses to provide invaluable opportunities to demonstrate the beauty of His Kingdom. He has sent us into a self-centered culture where the masses are focused only on what they can get. Against this backdrop, Christian businesses have the potential to turn heads and cause men to stop and think. So how is it with you? Are you allowing the Lord to transform obstacles into witnessing opportunities, whether it's receiving too much change at the cash register or knowing the tool is underpriced at a yard sale? You can keep the change or pay $35 for the tool, but you will miss a tremendous opportunity to shine light into a dark world!

# PART FIVE
## *The Daily Details*

# *Absolute Integrity* 21

There is perhaps no greater test of cycling endurance than the Tour de France. First held in 1903, the original race went completely around the perimeter of France. But it was difficult to monitor the progress of competitors. Due to persistent cheating when cyclists were out of sight of the judges, the course was changed. The modern Tour de France lasts twenty-one days and covers up to 2,200 miles, many through steep mountains.

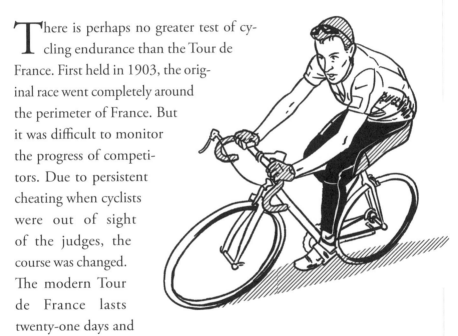

Among the cyclists who have competed in the Tour de France, none has been as successful as Lance Armstrong. From 1999 to 2005, the American won the race seven consecutive times. Lance Armstrong spent his early life competing in extremely challenging sports. At just sixteen years of age he began competing as a triathlete, and later he won national championships as a sprinter.

But in 2012 the United States Anti-Doping Agency charged Armstrong with using illegal performance-enhancing drugs. They announced that he was banned for the rest of his life from all competitive sports, and they stripped Armstrong of his seven Tour de France titles. Lance Armstrong had been accused of using drugs for years, but had always denied it. But finally in 2013, with mounting evidence too great to ignore, he went on public television and confessed to using drugs through those years of competition.

Without question, Lance Armstrong had incredible ability. He was able to focus year after year on challenging goals and achieve them. But all of that is forgotten now. Today he is remembered not as an inspiration, but as a fraud. In 2013, *Forbes* magazine published a list of the most disgraceful people of the year, giving out what they called "Integrity Disgrace Awards." Lance Armstrong was one of the "winners," and the article called him an Integrity Chump and a common cheat. Lance Armstrong, once a national hero, has become an embarrassment to the athletic community. Gone are the cheering crowds, the corporate sponsors, and the newsmen willing to do almost anything to get an interview with him. Today Lance Armstrong is retired, and talented as he was, he will always be known as little more than a swindler due to his lack of integrity.

We need to learn something from Lance Armstrong's story. A lack of integrity can blind the observer to all other virtues. Earlier, I shared my observations regarding the reputation of conservative churches and concluded that we tend to do well in honesty and integrity. We must not lose this virtue. Basic integrity is integral to the fabric of a Christian business. Lose that one thread, and the entire fabric will unravel. You can put up signs stating that you operate a Christian business, quote Bible verses on your business cards, and tell everyone you are a follower of Jesus. But just fall short in integrity once, and it would have been better if you had never let your relationship with God be known. If you don't follow through with what you promise your customers, don't bother handing out religious tracts. Without basic integrity, your efforts will do more damage than good.

So what is integrity, and how does it apply to business life? In this chapter I would like to look at several areas where I believe we have room for improvement.

## Follow-Through

I have worked with business owners who seemed so focused on finding the next customer that they gave little thought to the satisfaction of the last. Few things make or break your reputation more quickly than your level of follow-through. A boss who lacks follow-through can place tremendous stress on his employees. Recently I received a phone call from an employee of a small business. His job was to go out and sell projects, but he had lost confidence in his employer. He knew from experience that much of what his boss was telling him to promise would not be performed. So much of the company's energy was being poured into sales that there was little left for customer support.

Making the sale is exciting, and effective marketing requires time and energy. But a company that doesn't ensure that its customers receive at least as much as they were promised lacks basic integrity. The Psalmist David described the kind of man God approves as one who "sweareth to his own hurt, and changeth not."[a] This is a man who makes a promise, and even if following through causes him to lose money, he does not change his commitment. He considers his testimony and his word more valuable than money.

A lack of follow-through in business often stems from a lack of trust in God. We forget that He has promised to be with us, and suddenly the Kingdom of God and our testimony isn't as real as the money we might lose. But when our goal is for our business to be a public demonstration of what the world of commerce could be like if everyone followed Jesus, follow-through will occur naturally.

## Government Regulations

No matter what business we are in, we will need to interface with government on some level. Most of us have dealt with frustration over government regulations, and I am no exception. I have vivid memories of standing at building department counters trying to make sense of random codes I was supposed to comply with. I recall ill-qualified inspectors, who I suspected wouldn't know which end of a hammer to use, pulling out obscure regulations and insisting that I comply.

---

[a] Psalm 15:4

Sometimes it was something simple, but other times it was something that had no benefit to the structure, entailed a lot of work, and cost hundreds or thousands of dollars.

Building-inspector jokes abound at lumberyards. I have had to back up many times and examine my attitude toward government officials. Is it really possible to share jokes at the lumberyard counter while still honoring them, as the Apostle Peter commanded?[b] Can we mock those in civil authority while honoring them as Paul instructed the church at Rome?[c] And have you ever considered what our society might be like without government officials?

I remember driving down a newly refurbished street in Port-au-Prince, Haiti. It was nice to finally get onto a road without potholes, and the fresh asphalt was a joy to drive on. But there was one problem. The manhole covers were missing. Despite the absence of potholes, the driver had to stay alert if he didn't want his tire sunk in a manhole.

Why were the covers missing? It is possible, but unlikely, that they had been stolen, since they can be locked down. More likely it was a lack of government oversight. The contractor was likely able to buy off those who were responsible for placing manhole covers, and he moved on to the next project. In the developing world this kind of chaotic undercover business activity is normal.

So while we get frustrated with seemingly endless regulations, much of the world could use a few more. Restaurant owners get tired of government officials looking over their shoulders, but because of that very government oversight, we can frequent any eating establishment and eat without fear of food poisoning. Builders become weary of regulations, but because of them we can walk into public buildings without wondering if there is enough rebar in that overhead concrete structure. This is not the case in much of the world.

But beyond government oversight providing some benefits, consider the potential opportunities as we interact with officials. My experience has been that, while some can be difficult to work with, most

---

[b] 1 Peter 2:17

[c] Romans 13:1–7

are understanding. If you work cheerfully with them, it can be a good experience. Ask about their families and show interest in their lives. Few people welcome them with open arms. Show them what their job could be like if everyone followed the Lord Jesus.

I am alarmed when I hear of believers employing creative ways to ignore government regulations. Some put misleading labels on health food products to avoid monitoring by the FDA. Others circumvent regulations by publicly advertising that their raw milk is "not for human consumption," when in reality that is exactly what it is for. Perhaps our government is too restrictive and even misguided. But I am concerned when we become more passionate about health and conspiracy theories than about honesty, transparency, and the Kingdom of God. The Apostle Paul told us clearly that the Kingdom of God is not meat and drink.[d] We do great damage to our public testimony when, whether chasing health or wealth, we align ourselves with anti-government factions.

Our country has been blessed in so many ways. In light of what believers in other countries have endured, we should be thankful and eager to abide by the rules we have been given. But when we skirt building codes or other regulations, avoid truck weigh stations, or falsify driving logs, we bring reproach on the name of Christ. Though there are requirements, such as some OSHA regulations, where compliance is difficult if not impossible, followers of Jesus will be known for trying to comply whenever possible.

### Punctuality

History tells us that George Washington was punctual. One day his secretary was late for a meeting, and when he finally arrived, he blamed his lateness on his watch. "Then you must get another watch," Washington quietly replied, "or I, another secretary."[1] Washington understood that if you can't trust someone to arrive when he said he would, you probably can't trust him to follow through with other things either. Punctuality tells a lot about a man, and a habitual lack of it reveals a deficiency in integrity.

---

[d] Romans 14:17

Most of us have worked with someone who is habitually late. It seems, regardless what time the appointment, something comes up at the last minute. After this happens a few times, you conclude that it is most likely a lack of planning and integrity.

As the saying goes, we never get a second chance to make a first impression. And few things ruin a first impression like tardiness. If you say you are going to be there at a certain time, then be there.

> **We never get a second chance to make a first impression.**

It amazes me how people who would never think of stealing things somehow think nothing of stealing time. In the book of James we read, "But let your yea be yea; and your nay, nay."[e] Do what you said you would do. Follow through with commitments. Let your business and your entire life be known for integrity, even down to arriving on time.

### Conclusion

Our society is rapidly losing integrity, but against this dismal backdrop the Kingdom Christian is called to shine. There are some wonderful stories of believers who are demonstrating integrity in their business dealings. Recently I heard of a couple who received and accepted an offer for the sale of their home on a Friday afternoon. It was just a verbal agreement; no papers were signed. Over that weekend they received several higher offers. One of those offers was $50,000 higher than the original, and the would-be purchaser who had made the verbal offer became anxious when he heard the news. He couldn't afford to pay $50,000 more than he had offered.

But he needn't have worried. The sellers were people of integrity, and they informed the buyer they would stand by their original agreement. They had agreed to sell for a certain price, and that was the end of the discussion. Their integrity was worth more to them than $50,000.

How much is integrity worth to you? If you are serious about using your business to point others to Jesus Christ, integrity is essential. It dare not be compromised.

---

[e] James 5:12

# *Dealing with Employees* 22

In 1972 Pittron Steel was on the verge of disintegrating. The Pennsylvania company was in trouble financially, and tension between labor and management was at an all-time high. Pittron was a filthy place to work, and the employees felt little respect from management. Finally, in October the men felt they had endured enough and chose to strike. The resulting bitterness, charges, and countercharges resulted in what was called "eighty-four days in hell."[1]

Just before the strike, an employee named Wayne Alderson had been promoted to vice president of operations, and he had some unusual views regarding management. He believed the company's policy of managing workers by confrontation and intimidation was counterproductive. So, against normal protocol, he began to meet with union leadership. He also began walking through the plants and engaging the workers in discussion. Slowly he built relationships. After the strike was over, he was in a plant watching men work and visited an employee known as the chipper. This man's job was to crawl into the large steel castings and chip away defects with a heavy jackhammer. It was the hardest and dirtiest job in the plant.

Wayne watched for a while and then told the man, "Let me have a crack at it." Removing his suit coat, he climbed into the casting and lasted all of three minutes. Upon crawling out, he conceded that whatever the company was paying the man, he was earning every penny of it. This story spread through the factory like wildfire. By his interest and actions, Wayne brought dignity to the least respected job in the plant, and he slowly broke down the antagonistic culture between labor and management that had plagued the company for years. As his relationship with the laborers developed, Wayne even introduced a weekly Bible study, meeting with any of the men who were willing to come. But more was changing than just relationships.

As a result of Wayne Alderson's efforts, Pittron's plants increased production dramatically. Over a 21-month period, productivity rose 64 percent. Chronic absenteeism, which had been around 20 percent, dropped to less than 1 percent, and product quality became the best in the company's history. During the next year, labor grievances went from twelve per week to one for the entire year.

Ironically, due to high profits, Pittron became attractive to investors and was sold by its parent company to a corporation that didn't appreciate Wayne's style of management. Looking out for the best interests of the laborers was just too radical for the new company, and Wayne was asked to change his management style and remove himself from the weekly Bible study. Wayne refused to do this, choosing rather to be terminated.

**Coming Alongside**

Wayne Alderson's style of leadership confirmed that coming alongside employees is more effective than pushing from behind. His experience demonstrated the tremendous power in communication and mutual respect. If you have employees in your business, how do you see them? Do you see them as steps on a stairway? Something you tread on to get where you want to go? Are they pawns on the business chessboard, designed to be moved around, enabling you to win financially? Or do you see employees as fellow workers in a bigger picture, responsible for one part of the project and you for another? Can you see them as fellow children of God, and your business as something designed to bring blessing into their lives?

Paul wrote to the church at Ephesus concerning employer/employee relationships. He started by instructing employees: "Servants, be obedient to them that are your masters according to the flesh, with fear and trembling, in singleness of your heart, as unto Christ; not with eyeservice, as menpleasers; but as the servants of Christ, doing the will of God from the heart; with good will doing service, as to the Lord, and not to men: knowing that whatsoever good thing any man doeth, the same shall he receive of the Lord, whether he be bond or free."[a]

Notice Paul's strong words to employees. Don't just make it look like you are doing a good job. Do a good job! Understand that you are not just working for an earthly boss; you are employed by and account-able to the Lord. Powerful words! An employee is accountable to God for his work ethic.

Paul goes on: "And, ye masters, do the same things unto them, for-bearing threatening: knowing that your Master also is in heaven; nei-ther is there respect of persons with him."[b] Did you catch that? Being an employer isn't any different, and it isn't really your business. Paul says to be careful how you treat your employees, because you are an employee as well, and your Boss—the actual Owner of your business—will hold you accountable for your actions.

In his letter to the church at Colosse, Paul expands on this thought: "Masters, give unto your servants that which is just and equal; know-ing that ye also have a Master in heaven."[c] He is telling employers to be careful when deciding how much to pay their employees and what kind of benefits to provide for them. Whether you are a Production Paul with many employees or a Larry Little with just a few, you are actually an employee as well, and your Employer is very interested in how you treat those in His business.

God has always been concerned with how we treat others, especial-ly those who are financially disadvantaged. In the Old Testament Law, God had sharp words for those who oppressed the hireling,[d] abused them physically,[e] or even took more time than necessary in meeting payroll.[f] In the New Testament James echoes this theme: "Behold, the hire of the labourers who have reaped down your fields, which is of you

---

[a] Ephesians 6:5–8

[b] Ephesians 6:9

[c] Colossians 4:1

[d] Malachi 3:5

[e] Exodus 21:20–27

[f] Leviticus 19:13

kept back by fraud, crieth: and the cries of them which have reaped are entered into the ears of the Lord of sabaoth. Ye have lived in pleasure on the earth, and been wanton."[g] As Christian businessmen who say that God is the ultimate owner, we need to give close attention to how we treat those under our care.

**Servant Leadership**

When we cheerfully relinquish control and agree with God that He owns everything, there really isn't any better term than "servant" to describe our position as business "owners." We are called to lead, but we are just as much servants as the employees under us. How can we keep this concept alive in the middle of all the daily demands and challenges?

I believe one essential ingredient is frequent intercessory prayer for those we work with. Pray for their spiritual welfare, for their families, and for their interactions with each other. As we give thought to their spiritual struggles and lift them in prayer each day, they will become much more to us than just employees. The playing field will be flattened and the hierarchy removed. They will become fellow travelers dealing with the same challenges we face.

**A Listening Ear**

As employers, most of us like ideas from our employees that make our business more productive. But they will share more productive ideas if we have first been willing to listen and be involved in their personal lives. God has given us a beautiful example of how to listen to those we have authority over. The Bible says, "The eyes of the Lord are upon the righteous, and his ears are open unto their cry."[h] Even though God has authority over us, He is still willing to listen. As employers, we are called to demonstrate this characteristic of God in our relationships with employees. Ask about their personal interests, their children, and how they are doing in areas of difficulty they have shared with you. Ask, not because a vibrant relationship with your employees might benefit your business, but because you care about them.

[g] James 5:4, 5
[h] Psalm 34:15

One factory owner I met put his office out on the plant floor where his employees could easily access him to discuss anything on their minds. His main office is in a different building some distance away, so this is an inconvenience, but he wants to be close to them. His business has over $30 million in sales each year, yet he told me, "My best day is when I can help one of them with a personal or family difficulty. It is so exciting to be able to share a Scriptural truth that blesses their lives!" This man is determined to listen to the hearts of the men he employs.

## Rewards

Some employees respond to verbal affirmation, and an occasional compliment means much more than a higher wage. Others see financial remuneration as the ultimate indicator of appreciation for their efforts, and even affirmative words are worthless if not backed up by monetary reward. It is important to discern what conveys appreciation to an employee, and building a good relationship with him can help an employer do this.

Many seminars and books provide instruction on motivating employees to produce while paying them as little as possible. Such teaching reveals a sole focus on increasing profit. But shouldn't a business built upon a Kingdom-focused foundation determine pay scale from a different perspective? I am not suggesting that we need socialistic businesses or that every employee should earn the same wage. But if God is actually the owner of our businesses, I think we need to ask ourselves some questions.

I have discussed income equality with many men and have listened to many frustrated employees. Many feel overworked and are resentful when they see business owners living an affluent lifestyle while paying their workers the bare minimum. Many owners openly declare that God owns their businesses and they are just stewards. But somehow, though they profess to work for God just like their employees, their lifestyles do not support their stated belief. "Maybe owners should make more because they are taking the risk," one owner of a large business told me. "But it isn't right for them to pay their employees as little as possible and then go to Florida and buy a second home." I think Jesus would agree.

So how much income disparity should there be between the business owner and his employees? I don't think there is a simple answer to this question, but employers should give it prayerful thought. Those who take risks are entitled to a reward for that risk, but how much more would the ultimate Owner believe is fair? And what about your use of time as an owner? Is it right for you to go out and play while your employees work to enable your life of pleasure? How does God see all of this? As a business owner, you need to prayerfully consider these questions, keeping in mind that you have a Master in heaven who is no respecter of persons.

There are other ways than increased pay to bless employees. One employer shuts his business down for two weeks during the summer. This is a busy time for him, and he loses profit by doing it. But he wants his employees to develop strong family bonds at home, and since school is out, it is a good opportunity for them to spend time with their children. Another employer shuts his business down from Christmas to New Year to allow his employees to spend time with their families.

Many employers take their employees out to eat occasionally on company time, just to express appreciation for their efforts and give them an opportunity to share ideas and provide input. I know of still other businessmen who allow their employees to use business equipment for personal weekend projects, or take their children with them to jobs when possible. And while it can be argued that the intent of these efforts can ultimately be to have satisfied employees and therefore bolster the company's bottom line, that isn't the complete story. Many of these owners are followers of Jesus and have a genuine interest in their employees' lives and welfare.

## A Time to Terminate

Just as there is a time to hire employees, there is also a time to let them go. Paul told the church at Thessalonica, "For even when we were with you, this we commanded you, that if any would not work, neither should he eat."[i] God intends that every able-bodied man work, and when employees neglect their labors or are unfaithful, there is a time

---

[i] 2 Thessalonians 3:10

to release them. But even in firing there is a proper way to demonstrate both grace and truth. The truth is, they have not performed as they should have and must be dismissed. But this needs to happen in love. Take time to listen to their side of the story. If the problem is a lack of aptitude for that task in your business, try to locate another place for them to work. It may not always be possible to accommodate them, but they shouldn't be able to say you didn't care about them.

Many people haven't been taught a good work ethic. Many have spent a good part of their lives sitting in front of some kind of electronic media and haven't prepared for the work world. You won't be able to help them all, and these situations can put a tremendous strain on an organization. But as you see yourself working in God's business and being concerned about the same things He is concerned about, you will find yourself becoming more interested in the souls of these struggling people. Sometimes termination will be necessary. Sometimes it may actually be a blessing to you and the employee. But do it carefully, prayerfully, and in a way that demonstrates the love of God.

**Conclusion**

Recently I was talking to a man who had been employed by a Production Paul for many years and had recently left to launch a small business of his own. The company he had left was large, and he and the owner were from the same church congregation. I was impressed by his testimony regarding his former boss.

"I really enjoyed working there," he told me. "He always treated us well, and it was a hard job to leave. He cared about more than just getting the work done; he also cared about us." It isn't easy to work and worship with someone year after year. Misunderstandings can easily develop. But this business owner focused on more than just the bottom line. He didn't view employees as inferior people to be used to gain his own selfish desires. This former employee looked back almost longingly at his time of employment there.

God has placed employees under employers not only to make companies succeed, but also to give employers the opportunity to develop the spiritual life of the employees. Getting a glimpse of this potential ministry can have a radical effect on our businesses. It will cause us to treat employees with respect and consider the relationship from their perspective. It also has the potential to increase production. Business owners and managers often fail to comprehend this, and continual conflict between management and labor has been the historical result. Labor strikes, violent picket lines, and constant tension between those who should be working together have been costly. But God intends that His people demonstrate something entirely different. When we understand it is actually God's business, our focus will be on blessing those working under us and using those relationships to further the Kingdom of God.

# *A Christian Salesman?* | 23

M y five-year-old daughter walked into my office recently carrying five rocks. These weren't just ordinary rocks. They were value-added rocks. They had been painted with bright watercolors. She announced that these rocks were for sale, so I asked her what the price was. "One dollar each," she replied with confidence, "because then I will have five dollars." Now, these rocks looked nice to me because I was her father. But I doubt that anyone else would have paid a dollar to own one. What she needed was a *really* good salesman.

Most of us have come in contact with people who can sell almost anything. But when you think of a salesman, what words spring into your mind? High pressure? Greedy? Pushy? Artificial? Have you ever heard a parent say, "I sure hope my son grows up to be a salesman"? Have you ever heard a sermon where the minister calls young people to a life in sales? Why not? Is marketing products incompatible with following Jesus? Is "Christian salesman" a contradiction of terms?

In a 2013 Gallup poll, people were asked which occupations they trust for honesty and ethics. While nurses ranked at the top, with 82 percent of those polled believing they can be trusted, only 9 percent would trust a car salesman.[1] For some reason, those involved in marketing live under a cloud of suspicion. This can be a problem for the business owner, since the survival of his business depends on sales, yet the very act of promoting his product evokes distrust.

Dishonesty in business transactions is not a new problem. The wise man observed what was happening in the marketplace and wrote, "It is naught, it is naught, saith the buyer: but when he is gone his way, then he boasteth."[a] When purchasing, the buyer says the item is worthless, but then he goes off to brag about the great value of the thing he bought at such a cheap price. Evidently honesty isn't just a problem for the seller.

While buying and selling undoubtedly provide great temptation, it is possible to do both with integrity. But it will take continual diligence. A businessman must frequently return to his foundational vision and ensure that his marketing plans are built upon integrity and a Kingdom-furthering vision.

In this chapter we want to look at some basic principles to consider in marketing. As we do this, let the Spirit of God challenge your sales techniques. For while marketing can bring a reproach on the Kingdom of God when Biblical principles are compromised, it also provides wonderful opportunities to demonstrate something beautifully different.

**The Challenge of Honesty**

A hardware store owner shared one of his quandaries in sales. "Often when someone comes into the store, I can tell they really don't need what I am selling. It might be an older lady who has a clogged drain. We go back to the area where we sell these products and look at the options. She is looking to me for advice, and I know some of the basic products she has at home will work just as well as the expensive drain clog remover she is considering. Should I tell her?"

What do you do when faced with situations like these? You need to sell your product, yet you suspect that purchasing it isn't in the best interest of the buyer. At such times the foundational principles your business is built upon are exposed, and these are good opportunities for self-examination. Do my sales techniques reflect the principles Jesus taught? Jesus said we should do unto others as we would want them to do unto us. Can I obey this while selling someone something they wouldn't want if they knew all the facts?

**Honesty's Side Benefit**

In November 2008 the stock for Domino's Pizza hit a record low

---

[a] Proverbs 20:14

of $2.83 per share. The economy was down, their pizza wasn't selling well, and the company was in a slump. But more alarming, consumers didn't like their pizza.

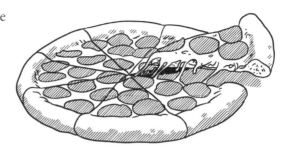

Disparaging comments and unflattering pictures were being posted on social media sites, and Domino's Pizza knew something had to change. So the management decided to take a bold and risky move. They decided to tell the truth.

They hired a marketing company and produced television advertisements that confessed they had an inferior product. They admitted that their crust tasted like cardboard and their sauce like ketchup, and they told the public they were going back to the drawing board and coming up with new recipes. They even invited customers to tell them more of what they didn't like about their pizza and promised to share these comments on their website. Consumers submitted over 40,000 pictures, with some of them saying Domino's pizzas were even worse than microwave pizza and "totally void of flavor." The company chefs took all this input and created a different pizza, asking the public to give them another chance.[2]

Marketing experts watched this and waited for it to fail. How can you tell people, "We fed you garbage in the past, but you can trust us now"? That's not how marketing is done. But in spite of the predictions of failure, it worked. The public loved this rare burst of honesty in advertising. Sales shot up, and by September 2011, Domino's stock was over $28 per share. In an interview the CEO of Domino's made this assessment: "The old days of trying to spin things simply doesn't work anymore. Great brands going forward are going to have a level of honesty and transparency that hasn't been seen before."[3]

Domino's Pizza was up against the wall and made a radical decision to try openness and honesty. And to the surprise of marketing experts, it worked! In a society where advertising agencies blitz the public with exaggerated claims, overstated results, and touched-up pictures, people find honesty and transparency refreshing. People are weary of false claims, and marketers are waking up to the fact that truth sells. As one author on marketing has said, "Truth is a powerful marketing tool. . . . It's not enough to talk anymore; the way to win is to use all of the means at your disposal to tell the truth."[4]

Honesty should be normal in a Kingdom-focused business, regardless of results. There may be times when telling the truth will cost us a customer. But increasingly, those in sales are discovering that while dishonesty may produce sales in the short run, over time honesty is still the best policy. Success in sales is a side benefit to consistent honesty.

### A Desire to Bless

A major pharmaceutical company asked business consultant Lisa Earle McLeod to shadow hundreds of their salespeople. This company wanted to find out what makes the difference between an average salesperson and a top performer. After just two days with one salesperson, without even examining the sales records, Lisa knew she had found a top performer. How could she be so sure? When this saleslady walked into a doctor's office, the receptionists stopped what they were doing and ran to get the doctors. This is not how doctors commonly react to drug reps!

Something was obviously different about this saleslady, but Lisa couldn't put her finger on what it was. On her last day with the woman Lisa asked, "What do you think about when you go on sales calls?"

The rep told her, "I always think about this particular patient who came up to me one day during a call on a doctor's office. I was standing in the hallway talking to one of the doctors. I was wearing my company name badge, so I stood out. All of a sudden this elderly woman taps me on the shoulder. 'Excuse me, miss,' she said. 'Are you from the company that makes drug X?'

" 'Yes, ma'am.'

" 'I just wanted to thank you,' she said. 'Before my doctor prescribed your drug I barely had enough energy to leave the house. But now I can visit my grandkids; I can get down on the floor to play with them. I can travel. So, thank you. You gave me back my life.' "

The sales rep told Lisa, "I think about that woman every day. If it's 4:30 on a rainy Friday afternoon, other sales reps go home. I don't. I make the extra sales call because I know I'm not just pitching a product. I'm saving people's lives. That grandmother is my higher purpose."[5]

This discussion had a profound impact on Lisa's study. She discovered that the seven top salespeople in this organization all had something in common—they had a higher purpose than just making money. At the end of the project, Lisa Earle McLeod wrote a book titled *Selling with Noble Purpose*. The saleslady who had so impressed her had been the top sales rep in the entire country for three years in a row. She wasn't going out each morning just to sell a product; she was on a mission to bless people's lives.

You need to sell your product or service to survive. Your business depends on it. But there should be a greater underlying motive than just increased sales. You need to believe that your product will actually bless the lives of your customers. If you aren't sure this is true, your message will not be believable, and perhaps you should look for another line of work. A follower of Jesus will have a foundational desire to market products or services that bless the buyer.

## Be Careful

One of my earliest memories of wrestling with the ethics of sales was at a church conference. The question arose whether it was right for a brother to be involved in selling real estate or in auctioneering. Some said that because these occupations are famous for exaggeration, the temptation to embellish the truth was just too strong, and a follower of Jesus wouldn't want to be tainted with this reputation. Others saw it differently. They said every occupation has its corresponding temptation. If a man is honest, he will be honest regardless of the temptation he faces, and if he isn't honest, his occupation will make little difference.

I was young, but I remember coming away with a realization that the area of sales provides strong temptation. While you can argue that an honest man will always be honest, and that God can enable a man to be faithful in any situation, we need to also acknowledge a basic truth. God has promised to give wisdom, and sometimes that wisdom tells us we are unsuited for certain occupations. We all struggle with vary-ing temptations, and if you find yourself fudging on truth to increase sales, find another line of work. It is possible to be a godly salesman. But the temptation to exaggerate or to hypocritically pretend you are best friends with potential customers is strong. And if one thing is clear from the life and teachings of Jesus, it is this: God hates hypocrisy.

There is also a difference between informing and pressuring. If you find yourself tempted to coerce clients, beware. Go back to your vision of building on a Kingdom-focused foundation. Do you really want a customer to look back with regret on his interaction with you? People will carry a memory of how working with you made them feel. You want your customers to desire to find out what motivated you to treat them with such genuine respect and honesty.

## Conclusion

President Herbert Hoover once said, "No public man can be a little crooked. There is no such thing as a no man's land between honesty and dishonesty."[6] While this sounds obvious, the reality is that in sales there is a strong temptation to create this no man's land. And if our hearts long for sales more than truth, we will struggle.

Some statements can be technically true yet not actually convey truth. The story is told of a pastor who moved into a new congregation, and one of his new parishioners brought him a pie. He tried eating the pie and it was terrible, so he threw it out. The next Sunday the lady asked the pastor how he liked the pie. "Oh," the pastor replied with a smile, "pies like that don't last long around our house!" The pastor's words were technically true, but the woman was left picturing some-thing less than truth.

The same is possible in sales. We can cleverly formulate sentences that may be technically true yet not convey absolute truth. But there is a way to avoid this, and that is to possess a genuine love for the client. If you actively pray and desire the best for each individual you transact business with, you will find yourself speaking absolute truth in sales. People will respect and seek out your business. Truth still sells!

# *Dealing with Debt* | 24

God's blessing seemed to be upon John's life and business. He had started out remodeling houses and then had his first opportunity to build a new house. The project had gone well, and he was amazed how much he enjoyed new construction over remodeling. Not only was it cleaner and easier, but it was much more profitable. Taking the profits from that job, John purchased a building lot and built his first house on speculation. The house was barely started when someone came along and wanted to purchase it. With the income from this, he was able to build two more.

For years John and his family had lived on a limited income, but now they began to enjoy the fruits of prosperity. As his small business grew, he delegated some of the work to employees, and he found himself with more time to work at home with the children. John continued to build and sell houses, and one day a real estate agent approached him. Some land that could be developed into housing lots was coming on the market. The agent was helpful, showing John how he could capitalize on this opportunity to take his business to a new level.

John went home that night very excited. Houses were selling well, he had a great team of men working for him, and the word on the street was that the market should keep climbing for several years. There was just one problem. John would need to go in debt to pull this off. He had never been involved with business financing before, and the thought made his wife uncomfortable. She liked the fact that business growth enabled John to spend more time with his family, but mortgaging their home seemed too risky. She felt they already had enough income, so why keep expanding? But John had been taught that if a business wasn't growing, it was going backward. John and his wife stayed up late that night. Finally, before they went to bed, she agreed to submit, and John proceeded with his plan.

He purchased the property, subdivided the land, and began to build. The first houses sold immediately. Encouraged by this, John hired more help and put up houses as quickly as possible. Then the market changed. Suddenly the phones went dead, buyers became scarce, and John knew he was in trouble. Housing prices continued to plummet, and within one year John was sitting across the desk from a loan officer again, this time to hear that the bank was repossessing his property, including his home.

When I talked to John, he was a broken man. Living in a small rental and working for someone else, he will spend many years paying off his debt. His life is filled with sentences beginning with, "If only . . ." "If only I hadn't tried to grow so fast. If only I had listened to my wife's intuition. If only I hadn't gone into debt." John had gifts to be a Larry Little. But he wanted desperately to be a Production Paul, and his desire to grow quickly drove him to take on more debt than was prudent. Consequently, John became one more on a long list of men who have discovered firsthand the deceitfulness and danger of debt.

### What Does the Bible Say?

You won't find a verse in the Bible that says that borrowing money is wrong.[a] In fact, Jesus gave us instructions on how we should loan money to others.[b] It doesn't seem likely that Jesus would encourage lending while considering the act of borrowing sin. But before we jump up and down and rush out to apply for a loan, we must come to grips with another Biblical reality. Every Biblical reference to borrowing is negative. If you go through all the verses dealing with the subject of debt, you will come away sobered with a realization that God never intended for borrowing to be the norm for His people.

---

[a] Some will point to Romans 13:8, but the context, in my opinion, seems to be saying we should live a life above reproach (see verse 7) and be sure all our debts are paid as we have promised.

[b] Luke 6:35

Most businesses today are fueled by credit, and debt is regarded as normal. Recently I read a short article by one of the foremost business advisers in our country. It confidently stated that credit "is the principal contributing factor to your business's future growth."[1] But in light of all the warnings in the Bible regarding debt, shouldn't Christian businesses be driven by more than just growth? Shouldn't the fact that Scripture speaks so clearly and consistently on this topic have some bearing on our borrowing decisions?

Under the Mosaic Law there was a strong connection between debtors and slaves. Both debts and slavery were to be canceled in the year of Jubilee. Often the slave was being held because he was a debtor.[c] In that day, and in ours, men went further and further into debt until they found themselves in total bondage. We find men in the days of Nehemiah mortgaging their fields and homes during desperate times to put food on the table.[d]

Debt in the Old Testament wasn't something you became involved in under normal circumstances. Of course, the argument is that today's inflationary economy changes everything. If you aren't using other people or other people's money to work for you, you won't be able to expand a business. There is some truth in this argument, and a business loan can provide a tremendous jumpstart to a small business. Sometimes, especially during high inflation, borrowed money can provide great opportunity.

In ancient times men found themselves in debt and enslaved because of famine or, in some cases, poor management. But today I see business owners burdened under a huge load of debt, often simply because they have been taught to believe the popular notion that being in business and being in debt are synonymous.

### Dealing with the Myth

One of the common assumptions in our credit-driven culture is that you can't operate a successful business without debt. But many successful businesses carry no debt on their balance sheets. In 2014, *USA Today*

---

[c] Deuteronomy 15:2–12

[d] Nehemiah 5:1–4

**179**

issued a list of twenty-six corporations on the Standard &
Poor's 500 Index that carried no long-term debt.[2]
Interestingly enough, one of
these mammoth corporations
was VISA Inc.! I wonder what

> **What we don't generally hear is how difficult it is for a business without debt to go broke.**

they have learned in the marketplace that has encouraged them to avoid
debt? Yet many seminars, books, and even accountants continue to encourage business owners to regard debt as a necessary part of business.
Sometimes small businesses are encouraged to stay in debt simply to
avoid taxes. But what we don't generally hear is how difficult it is for
a business without debt to go broke. Crushing debt is almost always a
factor when a business goes under.

So what are we to do with debt?

### Debt as a Dangerous Tool

Painkillers can be extremely useful. When your dentist removes an impacted tooth, you are glad he has certain drugs at his disposal. After
you return home, that little bottle of painkillers is precious and helpful. It has the ability to dull the symptoms and make life bearable for
the next few days. But you understand, even as you take the pills, that
this isn't something you want to do long-term. Every drug has side effects, and your goal is to reduce your dosage and move beyond need-
ing this medicine as soon as possible.

Debt has some similarities to painkillers. It can be useful in business,
but your goal should always be to reduce your exposure to debt and to
be free of it as soon as possible. Just as painkillers can dull you to reality, so it is with debt. It is easy to ignore problems in a business when
you have a good line of credit and a friendly banker. But just as people
can, and do, become dependent on painkillers, so businesses can, and
do, become dependent on debt. And then there are the side effects.

### Debt's Side Effects

In Paul's letter to the church at Corinth, he gave them something to
consider regarding marriage and single life. "The unmarried woman

careth for the things of the Lord, that she may be holy both in body and in spirit: but she that is married careth for the things of the world, how she may please her husband."[e] Paul wasn't saying a woman shouldn't be married, but he wanted the church at Corinth to understand the side effects. His goal in telling them this, he went on to say, wasn't to make life difficult, but to enable them to "attend upon the Lord without distraction."[f]

Debt can have similar side effects. You will find it more difficult to focus on serving the Lord while trying to please your banker. As you try to prayerfully discern God's will for your business by reading Jesus' teachings, you will find it is much easier without debt. Carrying a heavy debt load has a way of coloring our reasoning. The writer of Proverbs said, "The borrower is servant to the lender."[g] Debt has a way of dividing loyalty. It can become a distraction to your focus on serving the Lord. Don't ignore the potential spiritual side effects of debt.

### Dealing with Creditors

If you are in debt and find it difficult to repay, you must give thought to your responsibility as a believer. Revisit your goals for your life and for being in business. Most men find it difficult to admit to having a business problem (or any other problem for that matter). If your reputation is more important to you than having a Kingdom vision, then you will probably fail to portray a clear Christian testimony in the process.

First of all, communicate with your lender. That can be a difficult phone call to make, but you must communicate. Lenders are aware that businesses go through difficult times. But there is no excuse for not communicating, and few things reveal more about the true character of a man than his willingness to confess failure.

Second, get counsel. Surround yourself with a few godly men you can trust. Be open about your mistakes and be willing to receive their advice. It is so easy to procrastinate on this one. None of us want to look bad, and in almost every case there is opportunity to point fingers.

---

[e] 1 Corinthians 7:34

[f] 1 Corinthians 7:35

[g] Proverbs 22:7

Be willing to meet with others and expose the areas where you could have made better decisions. You will find that other godly businessmen will appreciate your openness. Anyone who has been in business long knows there are risks, and we all make occasional mistakes in judgment. And remember this: the circumstance you are in, regardless how hopeless, is redeemable.

## Conclusion

I am convinced that many of our businesses would be debt free today if their owners had taken the time to prayerfully analyze their motives. It is so easy to be driven by ungodly business coaches, accountants, peer pressure, or even the prevailing winds of our credit-dependent culture. But I encourage you to carry a vision for living debt free. In some businesses, especially farming, operating debt free can be difficult. But don't let that reality extinguish your long-term goal. Many who previously were encumbered by a high debt load will verify that financial freedom is a goal worth pursuing.

Peer pressure doesn't stop in our teens, and many of us make poor decisions due to what other people might think. Men in particular have difficulty saying no to business opportunity and growth, especially when their peers are in expansion mode. But purposing to avoid debt can keep you from running down unwise paths. As you ponder whether or not to pursue expansion, remember the words of Paul: "But godliness with contentment is great gain. For we brought nothing into this world, and it is certain we can carry nothing out."[h]

---

[h] 1 Timothy 6:6, 7

# *The Use of Force* | 25

A group of conservative Christian businessmen had gathered for a meeting. At the conclusion I overheard two men who owned rentals discussing the challenges of being a landlord. One of the men evidently owned substantial residential property and was unloading some of his frustrations on the other. He talked about the lack of morals among his renters and how a person just couldn't trust their words. He concluded by sharing some situations where he had been "forced" to involve the law and evict some of these dishonest tenants.

The listener nodded in agreement and then commented, "Well, I don't think the Lord intends for us to just let people take advantage of us."

I didn't hear much more of the conversation, but I left pondering those words. Is that true? Does Jesus really not want us to let others take advantage of us? Can you think of anything Jesus said that would lead to this conclusion, in the Sermon on the Mount or elsewhere? Is there anything in the way He lived that might help us make this deduction? Was there ever a time when Jesus was being abused by others, and suddenly He stood up and said, "That's enough! I don't mind giving up some of my personal rights, but this has gone too far"?

At times Jesus spoke vehemently. He challenged the religious leaders of the day, publicly calling them hypocrites, fools, and even a bunch of poisonous snakes. He also took aggressive action, overthrowing the moneychangers' tables in the temple and driving out the men involved. But we never find Jesus defending His own possessions or personal rights. So, without any teaching that encourages us to use force to defend our rights, and no example of Jesus doing it, how do we come to the conclusion that Jesus wouldn't want us to let people take advantage of us? Even the Apostle Paul seemed unaware that we are to defend ourselves against those who would take advantage. "Now therefore there is utterly a fault among you," he told the church at Corinth, "because ye go to law one with

another. . . . Why do ye not rather suffer yourselves to be defrauded?"[a]

The two landlords in the discussion I overheard belonged to different church fellowships, and both would have been opposed to using guns or the courts to defend themselves. They understood the two-kingdom concept and should have had convictions against using force. So how could they come to such a different conclusion regarding rental property and evicting defaulting renters? Is business different from the rest of life?

This belief that force must occasionally be used in business is not uncommon. Many Christian businessmen I have talked to are a little sheepish about the topic. They acknowledge inconsistency in practicing one way when deciding whether to join the military and another when trying to stay afloat in business.

In this chapter I want to look briefly at several issues. First let's look at why we are tempted to regard business differently, and second, what a follower of Jesus is to do with the use of force in business. Collection agencies, lawsuits, mechanic's liens, repossession, bankruptcy—all of these are legal methods of applying force.

Throughout history followers of Jesus have refrained from using the courts to defend themselves or their businesses. Yet today I see

---

[a] 1 Corinthians 6:7

Christians waffling on this. Are there times when it is acceptable to use these legal instruments and methods? Or could the difficult circumstances that tempt us to use these legal channels be redeemed to further the Kingdom of God?

## Why Is Business Different?

None of us would want to say that Jesus' teachings don't apply to business practices, yet the evidence suggests that some feel this way. Part of the reason may go back to how we regard the difference between the Old Testament and the New. Modern Christians appreciate the teachings of Jesus and speak well of them. They inscribe His words on banners and bumper stickers. They talk about the importance of loving our enemies, but when a Hitler arrives on the scene, they find themselves in a quandary. They want to obey Jesus, but they also want to eliminate Hitler. Because church-going people in the 1940s wanted to stop Germany more than obey the teachings of Jesus, they took up arms and fought, using the Old Testament to justify their actions.

I see a parallel in our businesses. We know Jesus taught defenseless living, and we desire to be faithful to His teachings, but we also desire to be successful businessmen. The truth is, the greater of the two desires will ultimately dictate our course of action.

## Following Jesus Can Be Costly

Choosing to follow Jesus will often be financially costly. Jesus didn't promise that adhering to His teachings would create a large business admired by your peers. He just said, "Follow me." Pursuing Him may cost you money, time, and perhaps even your business. If you are not ready to put your business on the altar, don't call yourself a follower of Jesus. Jesus was clear. "Whosoever he be of you that forsaketh not all that he hath, he cannot be my disciple."[b] Jesus isn't saying you can't have a business or be a successful businessman. But He is saying that everything you own, including your business, must be subservient to His commands. Failing to recognize this will make it hard to determine which path to take when the heat is on.

[b] Luke 14:33

## What Should We Do?

With regard to the use of force to defend our possessions or personal rights, the teachings of Jesus are consistent. Not only are we not to fight back against the aggressor, but we should bless him. Ponder how these words might be integrated into your business: "If any man will sue thee at the law, and take away thy coat, let him have thy cloak also."[c] This teaching is utterly illogical to the business mind. He doesn't even address who was right in the lawsuit! This man might have no right to your coat, but Jesus doesn't even view this as worthy of comment. In light of Jesus' words, how can we use collection agencies, evict renters, become involved in lawsuits, and apply force with mechanic's liens? If we are actively looking for ways to bless everyone, even those who might be trying to take advantage of us, our businesses will look radically different.

There is a difference, however, between being the aggressor and being called into court to explain ourselves. Paul stood before the Jewish leaders and said, "Hear ye my defence,"[d] and later he stood before King Agrippa and others to give a powerful defense. We even see him appealing to Caesar. But we never find him involved in any kind of counter-suit or trying to use the law to retaliate against his Jewish oppressors. If we really want to follow Jesus in every area of our lives, there is plenty of teaching to help us discern.

## Redeem This Situation?

I remember a contractor who had occasional difficulties with accounts receivable. He had a large residential construction company, and even though he worked with a wealthy clientele, many of them were living above their means. As I watched how he tried to apply Jesus' teachings in these situations, I was impressed. I repeatedly saw him take them out for lunch and spend time listening to problems in their personal lives. He didn't always bring up the fact that they owed him money, and he was obviously concerned about more than just his accounts receivable. He cared about them.

---

[c] Matthew 5:40

[d] Acts 22:1

Often, but not always, they would finally pay. But I never saw any of his customers resent him in the end. They sensed he cared about more than just money and that his life was motivated by something higher. This is an example of redeeming a difficult situation. I have seen other believers choose the same path when dealing with a potential lawsuit. Rather than rushing to hire an attorney, they sat down and showed concern for the person involved. Admittedly, many situations are complex, and we may be called to interact with calloused people who are unapproachable. Some scenarios, like Reuben cutting down the wrong tree, may seem irreparable. Yet even the most impossible situation can be used to demonstrate a Christ-like spirit and further God's Kingdom. Consequently, with the Lord's help, every situation can be redeemed.

An Amish businessman ran into difficulty a few years ago. His finances were a mess, his liabilities were much greater than his assets, and many local vendors needed to be paid. So church leaders from his community met with this businessman and his vendors one evening. They discussed the problem and tried to resolve it. Some of the vendors agreed to reduce what he owed, his church brothers pledged some financial help, and a committee was assigned to provide ongoing support and accountability. The issue was resolved within a few hours.

Of course, word of this got out in the community, and a local lawyer was heard to marvel, "How is that possible? How can you fix a major financial crisis like that in just a few hours?" In his world this kind of a situation would have taken months and thousands of dollars in fees. But it is possible for the Lord to use difficult business situations to demonstrate the beauty of following Jesus.

### Reducing Exposure

When developing a microfinance program for developing countries, I knew the use of force to retrieve loans was off the table. It would be foolish to go into a country and teach them the blessing of living out Jesus' teachings in everyday life, and then ignore His words when difficulties arose. So what could we do? We found ways to reduce exposure. We looked for systems or methods that kept risk of dealing with refusal to pay at a minimum. That meant we had to be more selective when approving loans, get references, and create a system where borrowers wouldn't want to default.

In the same way, we should give thought to reducing exposure to risk in our businesses. If we are not going to use collection agencies, then we will need to be more careful in providing credit. This can be challenging. Not only does our conservative culture function with more trust than general society, but our desire for acceptance and success can eclipse our prudence. When Jesus sent His disciples out, He told them to be "wise as serpents, and harmless as doves."[e] They were to be known as harmless, but that didn't mean they should be naive. He wanted them to keep their eyes open, and when doing business, we should as well.

Embracing the words of Jesus may cause you to avoid some clients or potentially profitable investments. You may decide that the risk is too high and the temptation to compromise too great.

**Increased Debt = Increased Temptation**

Few things increase our temptation to compromise on the use of force like carrying high levels of debt. Pressure from a banker has a way of shifting our vision, and it is much harder to resist threatening overdue accounts if you have a large loan payment looming over you. Debt can cause us to shelve the teachings of Jesus for the moment, and we can be tempted to use the world's methods for a little while. We have looked at this before, but it needs to be restated. One of the best ways to reduce temptation is to reduce debt. It will make following Jesus much easier.

> One of the best ways to reduce temptation is to reduce debt.

**Conclusion**

Maybe this chapter has been difficult to swallow. Perhaps the use of collection agencies, lawsuits, and mechanic's liens has become so much a part of your life that you find yourself resisting the concepts presented. I understand. But before you walk away from the message in this chapter, go back and revisit the overriding vision for your business. What

---

[e] Matthew 10:16

are your real business goals, and do they include giving everyone who interacts with your business a fresh view of Christianity?

Or maybe you agree with the concepts. Perhaps these have been part of your church standards for many years. Understand that there is a great gulf between avoiding these tools because of your church's position and proactively redeeming difficult situations.

It is possible to obey the standards of your church on these issues, while still demonstrating an aggressive attitude. You can legally comply but still send out a clear message that the primary goal of your business is to make as much money as possible. But a follower of Jesus will radiate a different message. Men were sent to arrest Jesus, and they returned without Him. The Pharisees asked why they didn't bring Him, and their answer was, "Never man spake like this man."[f] It seems they were so amazed that they forgot why they went. Perhaps God intends for the response of men interacting in business with His followers to be similar. Maybe God intends for people to walk away from transactions saying, "Wow, something is really different about that man. I want to know more!"

---

[f] John 7:46

# PART SIX
*An Overarching Vision*

# *Does Size Matter?* | 26

As I have tried to discern the perspectives of many fellow believers regarding business, I have found a strong preference for small enterprises. In fact, I would say most of those I interviewed would identify with Larry Little. Most tend to admire a man who provides for his family and has a couple of employees. But if he keeps growing and eventually has several hundred employees, suspicion develops. Why is this? Why do we agree that God has given some men the gift of business administration, yet become suspicious when this gift blossoms and their businesses become large?

Earlier we looked at the fact that we see so few good examples. It is rare to see a Production Paul become successful in business while living in a home, driving a car, and choosing a lifestyle similar to that of his employees. Few financially successful men seem capable of living simply so they can share their wealth with others. But there are other fears as well. Some say big business is hard on family life. How can a man spend time with his children while managing a large business? How can a man be a good father while being a corporate president?

In almost every conversation, I hear a similar refrain. Few men are able to become financially successful while maintaining a godly vision. But what if we did see examples of this? In other words, is the fact that we have seen so few successes the only reason we should avoid owning large businesses? Are there any Biblical reasons for avoiding big business?

Let's look first at the issue of time and focus. Does a big business always take a man's focus away from his family and, ultimately, the Kingdom?

## Big Business

Fred is the owner of a large, lucrative business employing many men and operating in several states. Fred's business started small, but good management aided its growth through the years. Today it continues to expand. But having had the opportunity to interact with Fred many times, one thing is clear. Fred's primary focus isn't on business. His mind doesn't dwell on business success, and I know of few men who spend more time with their families. Fred has the ability to find good men and delegate responsibility. His real love and focus in life is the Kingdom of God.

## Small Business

Travis is the owner of a small business. He employs several men, and his business has provided well for his family. Travis started out working on his own, and over the last ten years his business has grown little. This hasn't bothered Travis. He has no desire to grow larger, and frankly, I think he would fear seeing his business grow. I have had opportunity to observe both Travis's business and his personal life. Just like Fred, Travis's primary focus is on serving the Lord. But there is a problem. Travis doesn't seem to have any extra time. I have heard him repeatedly say he wishes he could spend more time with his family or travel to bless others, but his business ties him down. Travis always seems to be behind on office work, racing to get a bid out or running behind schedule on a project. My perspective is that Travis is doing a good job and has satisfied customers. But his business, as small as it is, consumes more of his life than he would like.

After watching Fred and Travis for years, several things are clear. Both want to serve the Lord with all they have. I have seen how both men have used the resources in their care. While Fred has more assets, neither seems to have a desire to accumulate earthly treasure. Yet there are some major differences. Fred is such a good delegator that he has time to go help someone in need, while Travis with his small business is rarely able.

Paul told Timothy, "No man that warreth entangleth himself with the affairs of this life."[a] Sometimes we think of this verse as a warning against big business, yet Travis seems to be more entangled as a Larry Little than Fred as a Production Paul.

I mentioned earlier that there aren't many good examples in big business, yet there are a few. Most of us can think of people comparable to Fred and Travis. What are we to learn from them? I am not trying to promote large business or to say that the larger a business is, the more time you will have for family. Asking Travis to oversee Fred's large business wouldn't take care of the issue. Neither should we conclude that the larger a business, the less chance of becoming entangled. God hasn't given everyone the same gifts of administration or delegation. This example doesn't mean that Fred is more important or valuable to the Kingdom than Travis. Knowing these two men as I do, I can tell you that Travis has some important gifts that Fred lacks. But Fred does seem to have the gift of business administration. So does size matter?

**Greater Size = Greater Temptation**

I clearly remember that meeting. In preparing to construct a building on a university campus, we were having a typical pre-construction meeting with the university project manager and several of the larger subcontractors. The project was on a tight timeline, and as the general contractor, I was afraid keeping the project on schedule was going to be tough. I had never worked with this project manager before, but I could tell he would be difficult to get along with.

But the reason I remember the meeting is because I failed. This project manager made a vulgar comment during the meeting, using the Lord's name in vain, and I didn't speak up. I should have responded or rebuked him in some way, but I didn't, and I knew why. There was too much to lose. It is one thing to reprimand a project manager at a pre-construction meeting when the job is small. But this was a large project, and this man had the power to make my daily life as a contractor, and my financial life as a business owner, miserable. So I chose to remain silent.

---

[a] 2 Timothy 2:4

## Added Zeroes

Added zeroes in business provide an added temptation to fudge on principle, whether dealing with a customer in arrears on his bill, exaggerating during a sales call, or remaining silent during times when we should speak up. As I left that meeting, I knew I had succumbed to the pressure of money. This doesn't mean a person should never deal with large amounts of money, but it does mean we should be aware of the temptations that accompany it.

I can also think of times when added zeroes created added testimony. David was a building contractor doing a large project for a developer. This developer knew David was a follower of Jesus and opposed to using the court system to collect funds. So when David turned in a bill, the developer said money was a little tight, but next month everything would be fine. David wasn't sure what to do, but he was already into the project deep enough that he proceeded. When next month's billing came around, he couldn't get in touch with the developer, and when he finally did, there were more excuses. By this time David's work was completed, and all he could do was wait and hope. David never did receive the $200,000 he was owed, and it almost put him out of business. It took him several years to recover. This unscrupulous developer took advantage of David's convictions. David could have won a court decision easily, but his testimony was worth more to him than $200,000.

Many of us know stories of businessmen who were willing to be faithful to the teachings of Jesus even though they lost a great amount of money. Some of these stories have been passed around for years, and the reason they are repeated is simply because of the number of zeroes. If they had involved a smaller amount, they might never have been remembered.

## A Life of Its Own

As we consider whether or not size matters in business, we need to address the potential for a business to eventually take on a life of its own. When a business is small, potential losses can usually be recouped by cutting back somewhere or by asking others for help. But when a business grows, this becomes more difficult. "When our business was small," one Production Paul told me, "my wife and I could eat beans when things got tough. But now, it really doesn't matter what we eat. It is a large enough animal that our grocery bill is insignificant."

This might not be important when times are good and income plentiful. But when the economy goes south, suddenly size can matter. Few things destroy public witness like unpaid bills. When a large business is deep in debt and fails, a church community can sometimes do little to maintain a clear Christian testimony.

Several years ago I received a phone call from the church leaders of two young business partners who had acquired a large amount of debt. They had been using down payments from new projects to make payments on old debt, and now they were at the end of that road, unable to pay. The leaders of their small church were justly concerned and didn't know what to do. The church wanted to maintain a Christian witness in their community but didn't have the assets to cover the debt. This was primarily a situation of bad management without accountability, but the size of the business and debt made the situation much more difficult.

Larger businesses also make it more difficult to control your vision. It is one thing to have a clear vision for using your business to bless the Kingdom of God, but entirely another to transfer this vision through managers on down to the people interfacing with the public. As one business owner said, "When you get so big, you are forced to hire people who don't share your vision." Another said, "The larger the business, the more difficult it is for the owner to keep his vision clear all the way out to the edges."

### Addressing the Concerns

We have looked at several concerns regarding big business, and I am sure there are more. But we have also seen how larger businesses can be a blessing to our communities and churches. Many of us were first employed by a large business and learned some valuable lessons there. We have also seen the blessing of occasionally having their financial resources to draw from. So how can we address the concerns associated with big business while still benefiting from the blessing? And how can our churches bless these businessmen while surrounding them with the necessary safeguards to ensure they remain focused on the Kingdom?

This may be uncomfortable to some, but I believe the answer is in closer accountability.

## Accountability

Recently I was invited to meet with a group of Christian business owners who meet monthly to hold each other accountable to Kingdom principles. It was a mixture of Production Pauls and Larry Littles—men who understand business and its inherent temptations and have pledged themselves to transparency and accountability. I was impressed. They openly acknowledged the dangers in big business and have chosen to open their lives to each other to avoid those dangers. But I also left with some questions. Why isn't the church more involved? These men were from different church fellowships, and these meetings seem to fill a need not met in their local churches.

Most conservative churches know how to hold people accountable, and most have certain agreements, written or unwritten. We understand that if a fellowship is going to survive in our culture, there must be individual commitment to those agreements. But too often churches give little thought to accountability in business. Consider your own fellowship for a moment. How far could a brother in your church go in business before questions would be asked? Imagine a very successful businessman in your congregation. Year after year you watch his business expand. Maybe you hear he has bought more farm land or is building yet another store. Would someone lovingly meet with him and inquire about his vision? Would anyone have the right to inquire about his debt load? Do your leaders have the right to speak into his life? I have heard leaders say, "The church shouldn't be held responsible for repayment of business debt if the owner didn't ask for advice before he got in that deep." In other words, "Don't come running to us if you didn't ask advice before taking out that loan." Maybe this is right, but I believe the blame goes beyond the businessman. Knowing the great potential for loss of testimony, shouldn't the church be involved earlier? If we are serious about our Christian witness, shouldn't there be accountability before the debt is acquired?

## Financial Transparency

For some reason, even in fellowships where accountability is high in other areas, business seems to be off limits. But it wasn't this way in the early church. In the book of Acts we find high accountability and financial transparency.[b] The need of our day is more churches that are willing to look closely at how to utilize the blessings while holding owners accountable and protecting them from the dangers inherent to wealth.

I know of congregations that ask each family to share financial records with a deacon once a year. Living with an awareness that I am accountable to others for my financial actions can be a powerful way to maintain a Kingdom business focus. I know of other churches where members consult with the leadership before pursuing investments over a certain dollar amount. Some congregations ask members to reveal their debt load once a year. This enables church leaders to work with a situation of increasing debt before it becomes a major concern. These congregations are committed to paying their debts and maintaining a clear Christian testimony in their communities.

Maybe this sounds radical and is outside your comfort zone. Perhaps you have grown up in a setting where the only time someone's finances are discussed is when there is a major problem. But is that really best? Is this the picture we get from the early church in the book of Acts? I'm not saying a congregation should immediately ask its members to reveal all their financial information. In some situations this might not be healthy. But I am saying the church needs more transparency. Perhaps a congregation could start by simply talking about the issue in settings where individuals feel safe expressing their concerns and viewpoints. I understand that this can be difficult, but we need leaders who are willing to take the risk.

## Conclusion

Most of us understand that big business has inherent dangers. One of

---

[b] Acts 2:42–47 Acts 4:32–37 Acts 5:1–11

the early Christian writers said, "They who are occupied with much business commit also many sins, being distracted about their affairs, and not serving their Lord."[1] We should take note of the warning. With big business comes greater temptation and potential for distraction. But there is also potential for good and blessing. If we are going to be blessed by the positive without being overcome by the negative, we need to wake up to our need for financial transparency.

Too often the Production Pauls among us are either exalted or despised. We privately roll our eyes at the size of their businesses and then run to them when the church needs money. But we can do better. Businessmen need both encouragement and accountability. Let's acknowledge that God has given them gifts to be used. But let's also care enough about the souls of businessmen, our local congregations, and our public witness to provide accountability.

# *A Time to Prune* | 27

We have a few fruit trees around our property, and I eagerly anticipate picking that first peach or apricot each year. I like to walk around the trees, ensure they receive sufficient water and fertilizer, and keep weeds from growing too close. Harvest may be months away, but in all these activities there is a sense that the tree and I are working toward the same goal. The weather isn't always what I would choose, and the weeds keep pressing in, yet together we fight back against these enemies and produce fruit. We are on the same side of the battle.

And then comes pruning time. While the other activities are enjoyable, I find pruning difficult. The tree and I have labored to produce every branch, but if I am going to have good fruit and a healthy tree, some branches need to go. Something inside me always rebels. I stand there with the shears and debate whether I really need to take off much. I don't want to damage the tree, so I often don't take off enough. From what I've read, apparently most of us have difficulty removing enough. Phrases like, "When in doubt, thin it out," assure me that other would-be gardeners also stand in front of their trees wondering if they really need to remove so much.

## Pruning Is Hard

Business owners have the same struggle, and businesses that fail to prune strategically will have difficulty producing the desired fruit. Pruning means cutting off something that looks vibrant, healthy, and promising. This isn't easy in business. It might be an idea or concept you have been nurturing for years, or a part of business you really enjoy.

But whatever it is, if it isn't taking your business in a Kingdom direction, that branch needs to go. And that can be painful.

Several years ago I talked to a business owner who was going through a difficult time. The economy had slowed and his sales had suffered. As we looked at his overall business, one part was obviously consuming a disproportionate amount of his time, energy, and profit. Year after year, regardless of how much money and energy he poured in, this division lost money. But he was still enthused about this product, which he had designed himself. He liked to talk about it, looked for ways to promote it, and was sure profitability was just around the corner. His love for the product was blinding him to reality. But the truth was clear; the product needed to go. It was like a lovely branch that wasn't bearing fruit, and it needed to be pruned.

**Nature Produces Profusely**

Just as a fruit tree produces more branches than needed, the mind of an entrepreneur produces more ideas than are practical. Consequently, his business can begin to look like an unpruned tree—lots of nice branches but little fruit.

Alan is an unusual man. He seems to smell business opportunity. He can sense a need, visualize a solution, and create another business before most of us have even grasped the need. But Alan has difficulty understanding the need to prune. Although he has started many businesses, he can't seem to find enough qualified men to follow through. Accordingly, he is always struggling. Even as he is trying to fix one business because someone in management failed, he is starting a new one. He enjoys starting businesses and is good at it. But his business life would be much more productive if he could learn the art of pruning. Perhaps he needs a few brothers who care enough to reach out and speak into his life.

> Just as a fruit tree produces more branches than needed, the mind of an entrepreneur produces more ideas than are practical.

## Pruning with Purpose

One businessman best known for pruning is Jack Welsh. Jack became CEO of General Electric in 1981 and immediately began eliminating unnecessary layers of management. During the first years he went through every department's management team, analyzed everyone's efficiency, and slashed the jobs of the bottom 10 percent. He was convinced General Electric had entirely too many managers, and he was ruthless in eliminating hierarchy. Many looking on didn't see the need for all of this. GE was doing well before Jack came. Why mess with success? But Jack Welsh saw potential that others didn't, and as a result the company experienced tremendous growth and profitability. But it wasn't just pruning that made General Electric more successful—it was pruning with a clear goal in mind. All of these cuts were intended to move the company toward efficiency and profitability. Jack Welsh was famous for pruning with purpose.

Pruning must be done with a goal in mind. In his book *Necessary Endings*, Henry Cloud argues that a certain amount of pruning is necessary in business life. But it is also essential "to have a good definition of what we want the outcome to look like and prune toward that."[1] Having a clear vision and purpose is essential.

Jack Welsh focused on corporate profitability, but as a follower of Jesus, your business goals are larger. Whether you are CEO of a large concern or selling sweet corn beside the road, you want "your" business to further the Kingdom. It should bless others and your walk with the Lord. So how are you doing? Can you see spiritual fruit coming from your interaction with others in business? Is your business life competing against or complementing your spiritual life?

It is easy to see when someone else is ensnared by business, but have you ever asked others if your business life needs pruning? Are you willing to open yourself to your church leaders or other Christian businessmen in this area of your life? Or is your financial life off limits to your brothers in Christ?

Sometimes there is a strong push in church communities to be self-employed. Consequently, men who do not have the gift of business administration can feel pressured to own their own businesses. This can lead to continual frustration and financial struggle. If you suspect you might be in this group, look closely at your reasons for being self-employed. Is business administration your gift, or are you simply being driven by peer pressure? Pruning includes cutting off wrong motives and desires.

## Pruning with Proper Perspective

Whether you are pruning a tree or your business life, a proper perspective is essential. Every cut is made for a reason, and it is important to identify that reason before lopping off the limb. Before you prune too much from your business, or before you assume everything is fine and nothing needs to go, I would challenge you to get advice.

Ask someone who knows you well. Ask a few brothers within your congregation who may look at business from a different perspective. Sometimes it is much more comfortable to open yourself to a brother who views business just as you do. But we all have blind spots. If you are serious about using your business for the glory of God, prayerfully consider your business life from your brother's viewpoint. You may find areas to prune that you had never before considered.

Many of us fail to utilize one of our best resources—our wives. No one knows what moves you, drives you, and motivates you like your wife. If you are blessed with a godly, Spirit-filled wife, take time to listen to her counsel regarding your business. Ask her whether you are motivated more by financial profit or the Kingdom of God. Ask her about your allocation of time and whether you are giving sufficient attention to your children. I am not saying your wife should run your business, but be willing to prayerfully consider her perspective. You may have forgotten that you are simply a steward. A godly spouse can help remind you of this. Sometimes personal ambition and a desire for achievement need to be pruned.

## Conclusion

We usually end up with what we want most. If I want my fruit trees to produce fruit, then to the best of my ability I will prune away everything competing with fruit production. If everything else is in order, that tree will produce fruit. The same is true in business, and this is why it is essential to analyze what you want. Do you really want a close walk with the Lord and a business that furthers His Kingdom? Or have you drifted into a love for business itself and the financial reward it brings? Identify what you are striving for and then prune to reach that goal. You will need to pass by some opportunities and ignore some good deals. If you are a natural Production Paul, the most difficult pruning in your business life may not be deciding which division or product to eliminate. It may be the decision to downsize because of the impact business is having on your spiritual life. It may mean choosing to give up personal ambition, status, and the financial reward that continual business growth brings. These choices will be much easier if you have already agreed with God that it's not your business.

# *Business as Missions* | 28

Ken Crowell moved to Israel in 1969 with his wife and two children. Ken intended to start a business, be a Christian witness, and provide work for the local people. Since that time, Crowell has started a number of businesses, including Galtronics, a company that employs hundreds of Arabs, Jews, and Christians. The name Galtronics, Ken likes to tell people, is derived from Psalm 37 in Hebrew. "Commit thy way unto the Lord [*gol al Adonai*]; trust also in him; and he shall bring it to pass."[a]

For more than twenty years, employees at Galtronics have worked together to construct various electronic components, some of which are used by large corporations like Motorola and Samsung. Ken's employees give various reasons why they work at Galtronics. An article in *Christianity Today* reported, "They find substantial incomes and benefits, subsidized all-you-can-eat buffet lunches, and often, salvation through Christ." Crowell has opened new plants in China and South Korea as well, and from the beginning

---

[a] Psalm 37:5

has been clear about his motive. "The calling was first to go to an area where there was little or no Christian witness, to give employment to believers and nonbelievers in a safe working environment, and to support the building of a local church."[1] Ken Crowell passed away in 2012, and his pastor summed up his life like this: "He came here with this tremendous vision and no one thought it would work, and it worked because of his faith in the Lord Yeshua, in the Messiah."[2]

Ken Crowell is just one of many who have attempted to use business as a vehicle to carry the Gospel of Jesus Christ.[3] For years, most missionaries in foreign countries were sent and supported by their churches at home. But many missionaries came back asking if this traditional method was really the best way to reach the lost. Was it really giving a true picture of how the Gospel was to be lived out if the missionaries didn't have to work for a living? Were missionaries who were insulated from the daily need to provide for themselves really equipped to demonstrate what it meant to follow Jesus in everyday life? We know that much of Jesus' teaching revolves around money, the struggles of daily life, and how to properly interact with others. How can missionaries demonstrate this if they don't need to toil daily to provide for their families?

Then there are restricted countries. How can a missionary move to and live in a country where the government is opposed to Christianity? You can't just move to Iran and tell the Iranians that you are a Christian missionary. If you aren't working every day, you will meet a high level of suspicion. If you can't point to some constructive business you are involved in, you will soon be asked to leave. Out of these concerns, the concept of using business as a mission vehicle began to rise in popularity. Today Christians in many countries are using business as a way to reach out to the lost, and many indigenous churches have been planted as a result.

There are different approaches and differing opinions about which business models work best in each setting. Some missionaries take jobs in restricted countries, giving them a reason to be in the country and providing opportunities to reach out to fellow employees. Others have started small enterprises and use these legitimate for-profit businesses as reasons to be there. These small businessmen often refer to themselves as tentmakers, using the Apostle Paul as their example of working to support himself while evangelizing.[b]

Patrick Lai, formerly a traditional missionary, speaks of the added credibility that comes with using business as a vehicle in evangelism. "Tentmakers are viewed as contributors to society," he says. "Many non-Christian countries look at missionaries with disdain or distrust. However, tentmakers are seen as people who invest in the community by creating services, providing education, or employing people. This viability gives us respect, which opens doors among both government and religious leaders."[4]

While I have never met tentmaker-missionaries who would insist that using business is the only way to evangelize, they all agree that business can be a useful tool in spreading the Gospel. It places you right in the middle of daily life and provides an excellent opportunity to demonstrate how Jesus would respond in difficult situations.

### What If It Were You?

Imagine for a moment that you have moved to a foreign country. It is understood that, while your business must be profitable to survive, your overriding goal is to reach out spiritually to those you meet. Picture yourself performing your normal daily activities and facing the challenges you routinely deal with. How might living in a foreign country for the specific purpose of reaching out to others affect your business life?

Imagine calling the client who keeps promising to pay but doesn't. To remain in business, you must keep working with this person and remind him of his responsibility. Yet you are aware that threatening or becoming angry could undermine your purpose. Just a few hasty words could doom your mission. Or imagine calling the vendor who hasn't delivered that product on time, or who said he would show up yesterday and didn't. You must contact him, but would your voice on the phone sound different as you remember your primary goal? Think about interacting with suppliers. If you had gone to the trouble of moving your family and business to this foreign country to share the Gospel, would

---

[b] Acts 18:3; 20:33–35

you drive a hard bargain when purchasing? Your goal would be to have that supplier hang up the phone thinking, *Something is different about that man. Money doesn't seem to be his main focus. I want to know more about what motivates him!*

If your main purpose in a foreign country was to use your occupation as a platform to share the radical teachings of Jesus, you would look for opportunities to demonstrate this. You might look for mistakes in billing that favored you and expose them, even though it cost you. You would look for opportunities to bless the businesses of your customers. You would look for ways to help your competitors. Imagine the impact if you could walk into one of your competitors' stores and share techniques that could increase their efficiency. As a missionary, you would look for these kinds of opportunities. After all, showing people the Kingdom of God in work clothes is why you moved halfway around the world!

**A Business Opportunity**

Charles owned and operated a small residential construction company in which he worked by himself. One day Mr. Jones asked Charles to remodel his house. Charles looked at the project, estimated the expenses, and told Mr. Jones it would cost around $40,000 to do the job. Mr. Jones accepted the offer, gave Charles one-third of the amount up front, and the work commenced. After a good part of the project was complete, Charles billed Mr. Jones for the rest of the $40,000. Mr. Jones, who was pleased with the work and the price, paid immediately, and the project was soon completed. A few weeks after the remodel was done, Charles called Mr. Jones and said he wanted to come over to finish settling up. Mr. Jones said that would be fine, suspecting he would owe a little more money. After all, the price had been reasonable. He had enjoyed working with Charles, and if he owed a little more, he would be glad to pay.

Charles came that evening and told Mr. Jones that the project had gone a little differently than he had expected. He pulled out his ledger and showed Mr. Jones that he had gotten better prices on some materials and had spent fewer hours than estimated at first. Consequently, he refunded Mr. Jones $7,000, thanked him for the opportunity to do the project, and headed home.

I don't know if Charles ever told anyone about that evening or not, but Mr. Jones did! In the lumberyards I frequented, this story was hot news for a while. Businessmen just don't do that kind of thing, and it made all the other contractors scratch their heads. But think about the impact that $7,000 had on our community. Many men professed to be Christians, but Charles had found a way to demonstrate what following Jesus really looks like.

If you had moved your business to a foreign country with a goal of sharing the Gospel, wouldn't you look for opportunities like this one? Of course you would! You would be foolish to pass up the potential of a situation like this. Charles could have made at least $7,000 more on that project, and everyone in our community knew it. But Charles, like Jesus, was thinking about Mr. Jones as well. He wanted Mr. Jones to win. And the Lord used this event to showcase something of much greater value than $7,000.

**Must Missions Be Foreign?**

Does business as missions work only in other countries? Must we cross water and travel to some far-off country to be a tentmaker? Of course not. We talk about methods of reaching out here in a developed country and how difficult it is to get anyone interested in the Gospel. This country is saturated with materialism, and our neighbors are on a quest for yet more. How can we get their attention? Is the answer more tracts, more signs, or more programs? There is a place for these, but we might be missing something. What if we started demonstrating something radically different in our businesses? Paul encouraged the church at Philippi to live their lives "without rebuke, in the midst of a crooked and perverse nation, among whom ye shine as lights in the world."[c] Live differently from those around you!

Maybe you have a hard time visualizing your business as a mission. Perhaps in your mind mission work is just telling, giving, and proclaiming. But I propose that you rethink missions. What is the net value

[c] Philippians 2:15

to the Kingdom of God when a businessman chases the dollar just as hard as everyone else, mentally justifying this pursuit by giving to "missions"? How much more could be done if we would simply apply the teachings of Jesus to our everyday lives and businesses?

Greg owns a small plumbing business. As he came to a job site recently, a man approached him and said, "Hi, Greg, do you remember me?" Greg said he didn't, and the man went on to tell his story. Twenty years ago this man had been a forklift driver on a job where Greg was working.

"I don't think I ever asked you any questions, but I watched how you talked, worked, and interacted with others. There was something different about you and the way you did business, and I knew you had something I wanted. I knew you were following Jesus, and I went home intent on following Him as well."

A tear ran down Greg's cheek as he told me, "Today that man's entire family is serving the Lord. I didn't even remember this man or have any idea he was watching."

What if this kind of story were normal? What if the church today was known for doing business differently? What if more people saw Jesus through our businesses and walked away wanting to serve Him too?

**Conclusion**

We underestimate the potential in business. Consider the country of Indonesia. Christians have sent traditional missionaries there for hundreds of years. In spite of all the mission activity, that country has the largest concentration of Muslims anywhere in the world. How did the Islamic faith gain such a foothold? Was it because Muslims had a vibrant mission plan? Have they poured large amounts of money into their mission programs? No, the country was evangelized to Islam years ago primarily through traveling traders and businessmen. I was told by one man in Indonesia that when the Christians came, they isolated themselves in mission compounds, having little daily interaction with the local people. The Muslims, on the other hand, worked with the common people and became involved in their daily lives. These men came to do business, and in the process told the people about Mohammed.

As you consider your business, rethink the possibilities. God has more in mind for your business than financial gain. Perhaps His vision for your business is greater than you have ever imagined. Maybe He sees more potential than just using your business as a money-producing machine. Consider using your business as a mission.

# *Our Reference Point* | 29

Few companies in modern history have enjoyed such spectacular growth as Enron Corporation. Launched in 1985, it was the darling of mutual funds and the talk of Wall Street investors by the late 1990s, and woe to the retirement account that failed to include its stock. Beginning as a pipeline company, Enron profited by transporting natural gas from suppliers to utilities and businesses. But all this changed when, due in part to lobbying from senior Enron officials, the electrical power markets were deregulated. Enron began buying and selling electricity as a broker. But instead of bringing buyer and seller together as a traditional broker, they entered into contracts with both, making a profit on the difference.

Enron developed increasingly complex contracts and hired experts in mathematics and economics to help manage Enron's risk. The company profited tremendously. Since Enron was considered a "safe utility stock," investors, seeing high returns with little risk, purchased the stock in huge quantities, driving the stock price continually upward. As money flooded in, Enron's products and services became more complex, and Enron formed a large number of partnerships and subsidiaries. This allowed managers to shift debt off Enron's books, making the company look even more enticing to investors. By the year 2000, Enron had approximately 20,000 employees, claimed annual revenues of over $100 billion, and was considered a well-managed company. *Fortune* magazine even named Enron "America's Most Innovative Company" for six consecutive years.[1]

Like most large companies, Enron had extensive corporate policies. In July 2000, Enron presented a sixty-page code of ethics to its employees, the introduction signed by Chairman Ken Lay himself, stating that every employee must conduct business in accordance with the highest ethical standards.[2]

Even as employees were reading this call to a high standard, upper management was involved in one of the greatest business conspiracies the world has ever known. Once the shell game was exposed and the company's actual value made known, Enron's stock dropped from over $90 to under $1. On December 2, 2001, the same year *Fortune* had proclaimed it "America's Most Innovative Company," Enron declared bankruptcy, sending all 20,000 employees home.

How could this have happened? How can an innovative and safe utility company be hollow underneath?

It happened because those at the top began to use profit as their reference point. In spite of their bold written standards regarding the importance of sound business ethics, they were actually guided by something else. The name Enron is still well known today, not for innovation in business, but for scandal, dishonesty, and fraud.

**What Is My Business Known For?**

Over time every business becomes known for something. Customers interact with it, employees come and go, and the business gradually gains some kind of reputation in a community. What are people saying about businesses owned by members in our conservative churches? More important, how do our businesses reflect the Gospel of Jesus Christ? I believe all of us want our businesses to point others to the Kingdom of God. We may even have this in our printed vision statement. But is it possible to call our companies Christian when little about them demonstrates the Jesus we claim to follow? Hypocrisy is a real temptation in our lives. One of the major messages in the Bible regarding the final Judgment is that hypocrisy in professing believers will be exposed.[a]

How can we ensure this doesn't occur in our businesses? What steps can we take to be sure our stated goals, unlike Enron's, are actually lived out? If we are going to avoid hypocrisy, we must examine frequently the primary reference points that guide our business decisions.

## Pragmatism

Most of us, over time, develop a sense of what works and what doesn't. Since we like things to run smoothly, it is easy to gravitate toward using what works best as our primary point of reference. If one of our main reasons for crawling out of bed in the morning is to make money, it is easy to view any business practice that increases profitability as good. Anything that doesn't increase income is bad. I don't think we realize how easily this idea creeps into a business culture.

Stop for a moment and consider your business. Have you drifted into a pragmatic view? Are you tempted to fudge the numbers just a little to save on taxes, or give a higher estimate when you know a client isn't likely to get another bid? Would you bargain for the best deal even when you know you are cheating the seller? Is it easy to stretch the truth in your advertising?

If you answered yes to the above questions, you have the pragmatic thoughts of one who is driven by the financial bottom line. To be free of such thoughts, fully commit your heart to truth and the Kingdom.

Let's look at some more reference points businessmen use in making decisions.

## Common Business Practice

One reference point is common business practice, or the industry standard. These are methods of operation considered normal, moral, and ethical for your type of business. But common business practices change over time and differ between cultures.

I recently talked to a man who had lived in Ukraine. Many

---

[a] Matthew 25:31–46

businessmen, he told me, use cash and do not report their income. This has become so normal there, even among professing Christians, that it is considered a common business practice. There is so much disrespect for government and laws (some of which contradict each other) that cheating on tax returns seems justifiable. And bribery, something frowned upon in much of the developed world, is common business practice in much of the developing world. Without a little extra cash to lubricate the process, things just don't happen.

In America it is common for people to avoid sales taxes by reporting a lower dollar amount on a used vehicle title than what was paid in the transfer. Others hire their laborers as subcontractors to avoid paying taxes or benefits. Paying "under the table" to avoid sales and income taxes also occurs, sometimes even in conservative communities. If our decisions are based on ever-changing common business practice rather than on the unchanging truth of God's Word, we can fall prey to these deceptions.

## Higher Ground

Earlier we looked at using the teachings of Proverbs as the primary reference point in our businesses. This approach is common in most Christian business teaching. Honesty, diligence, saving for future need—these themes are popular in most Christian business seminars, and they work. These are the building blocks of material wealth. The book of Proverbs describes what is just and right, and many today believe they are operating their businesses by Christian principles if they simply adhere to the teachings of Proverbs.

But Jesus calls His followers and their businesses to higher ground. Remember, the principles in Proverbs were true when they were written, they were true when Jesus was on this earth, and they are still valid today. Following Proverbs produces profit. But Jesus calls His followers above mere earthly profit. Jesus didn't say you couldn't gain a fortune by heeding the Old Testament. He just taught something of infinitely greater value. When you make the teachings of Jesus the reference point for your business, sometimes you will need to surrender what is fair and right, and even the common sense principles in Proverbs.

Consider for a moment the financial situations Jesus addressed in His teachings. Think about the man who wanted his brother to divide the inheritance with him,[b] the rich man who took satisfaction in the reward of his diligence as he built greater barns,[c] or the rich young man who apparently lived an upright life and had great possessions. Can you find anything in the Old Testament that says it's okay to divide an inheritance unfairly? Does it say it's wrong to build more barns? Does it teach that a man should sell all that he has and give to the poor? Of course not. Jesus' teaching was radical—a new reference point for those who were well instructed in the Law.

Jesus' teachings about finances were a call to higher ground—much higher ground! So what did the early followers of Jesus do with this? We barely get into the book of Acts, and the church was putting this into action. Notice these words: "And the multitude of them that believed were of one heart and of one soul: neither said any of them that ought of the things which he possessed was his own; but they had all things common. . . . Neither was there any among them that lacked: for as many as were possessors of lands or houses sold them, and brought the prices of the things that were sold, and laid them down at the apostles' feet: and distribution was made unto every man according as he had need."[d]

What was the early church's primary reference point? The teachings of Jesus. They weren't making financial decisions based on what was common practice, or even going back to Proverbs and applying common sense. They were excited about the new investment opportunities they'd never understood before. Their primary focus was the Kingdom of God, and their financial decisions were based on that point of reference. The early church, like Jesus whom they were following, was calling people to higher ground!

**Your Primary Reference Point**
So what is your primary reference point when making business decisions? Sometimes it is hard for us to analyze our own selves and our

[b] Luke 12:12
[c] Luke 12:16–21
[d] Acts 4:32, 34, 35

businesses. But rest assured that those you interact with regularly know whether following Jesus is actually what drives your life and business.

Years ago I developed a close relationship with a manager at a local lumberyard. He was an unbeliever, yet he had many questions about faith. He believed "something was out there" and was familiar with Jesus' teachings, but he wasn't convinced that God had created the world. One day as we were talking about some of his struggles, he said, "Many professing Christians come into this store. Some habitually pay their bills late, some complain about everything, and some treat our employees like dirt. It doesn't take long, when you're doing business with someone, to find out whether or not they actually believe what they profess." Even though this man wasn't ready to proclaim Jesus as the Son of God, he knew hypocrisy when he saw it. He could see what we are so often blind to. It is one thing to say you own a Christian business, and another to actually use Jesus' teachings as a primary reference point.

**Conclusion**

I suspect the senior officials at Enron had no clue how far the path would take them the day they first began fudging with honesty. Even though their stated code of conduct proclaimed their desire to uphold the highest business ethics, they didn't practice it. In their pursuit of profit, they lost sight of ethics and basic honesty. This happens easily in a business, so we must frequently go back and examine our primary reference point. Many have found value in writing a vision statement to articulate the company's goals. A mission statement describes how the company plans to achieve the goals within their vision statement. It describes what a company does, and how it intends to do it.

One of the business owners I interviewed shared his company's vision statement. It stated that the company's first goal is to "finance the work of God's Kingdom and seek to aid in alleviating the suffering of the poor." This is a family-owned business, and they haven't shared their mission statement with the public. But they feel it is essential to have something in writing that they could refer back to when making decisions. If you are self-employed, I encourage you to write out your vision, and be sure that your primary reference point is Jesus.

# *What Would God Want Me to Do?* | 30

Andy and his wife met me at the door of their large Amish farmhouse and graciously invited me in. Their six children were working and playing cheerfully outside, and their simple home was calm and inviting. I explained that I had been interviewing Christian business owners, and someone named him as an employee who demonstrated a Kingdom focus through his occupation. Just a few minutes into the conversation, I understood why his name had been given to me. As a manager for a large cabinet company, he is responsible for about forty men. He expressed a desire to use his occupation for the Lord, sharing some of his inner wrestling.

"We build these fancy cabinets, and sometimes I wonder if I can really bless people through what I am doing. But I have finally decided I can. It's not by giving them larger kitchens than they really need, but by working in an ethical way and giving them more than they expect."

He went on to describe his great opportunity at work as he interacts with others. "My goal is to bless and positively influence the men under me. I teach them that we are in the business of helping other people. Whether customers, vendors, or whoever else is observing, our actions should challenge people who see how we do business."

Andy told me about one employee who was living an immoral lifestyle, was always disgruntled, and had no vision for the future. Andy began spending time with him and placed him in a different work role that better fit his skills. "He just began to blossom!" said Andy with obvious excitement. Today, that man is happily married, has a son, and is trying to lead a godly home.

I was impressed, but also curious. Andy was an intelligent man, had a good grasp of business, and obviously could manage men. Why didn't he have his own business, where he could make a higher income? He seemed a perfect candidate for self-employment. So I asked why he was working for someone else.

"I have considered going on my own several times. But I have analyzed my abilities, and I believe my gift is helping someone else accomplish his vision."

Andy was content playing second fiddle because he believed this best used the gifts God had given him. He intrigued me. Here was a Servant Sam who was excited about the possibilities in large businesses. I was also fascinated by his honest assessment of his abilities. He seemed much more interested in finding his place in life than in maximizing his income. He talked about the challenges that come with wealth and the impact it has had on his church community.

"We have not been intentional enough. The Amish come from an agricultural background where there wasn't much surplus money at the end of a year. When the switch to business came, our people gave little thought to what we should do with the extra resources."

So I asked Andy if he knew any large business owners in his area who were obviously using their daily business life and resources for the Kingdom. Andy thought for a moment.

"Not many. It seems that most men, even in our conservative churches, primarily use business profits to fund selfish pursuits. Very few employers live at the same level as their employees, but I would have to say my boss comes as close as I have seen." I had never met Andy's boss, but I knew he should be my next stop.

### Business as a Platform

"Business for me is a platform for taking Jesus to the marketplace," was David's first comment when I asked about his business vision. "We try to do this at work in a variety of ways, but that is our ultimate goal." David, Andy's boss, is a Production Paul. His business is profitable and continues to grow, yet it was obvious as we talked that his primary focus wasn't on profitability. "I believe in making a profit," he said. "Without profit I can't continue to function. But my primary goal is to develop men who can have a positive impact on our community."

David has nearly one hundred employees, and his goal is to see each of them develop into godly leaders. He sees a great need for men who are willing to take their Biblical place as leaders in their homes, churches, and communities. To accomplish this, he meets regularly with his managers to study the Bible and to encourage each other. David has developed teaching materials for these meetings, and employees are paid to attend. His aim is to see them draw closer to God personally and then go out in the shop and model the leadership skills they have learned. David's business is large enough that his employees come from a large geographical area. He wants to see his men return home, apply what they have learned, and be salt and light in their communities and churches.

David has a natural ability to administrate business. His company is growing rapidly, he has an expanding satisfied customer base, and the business has been profitable. He has developed a vision and articulated it clearly to his employees. Yet this vision is worthless without men like Andy. David needs men who are able to put feet under his vision and put it into action. David understands this and speaks highly and respectfully of the men like Andy who work with him every day.

I came away from interviewing Andy and David with a clearer picture of how businesses could further the Kingdom of God. God has given these two men different abilities, yet each admires the gifts in the other. Because each has respect for the other's gifts and a greater motive than personal gain, their abilities are meshing to the glory of God. David summarized by saying, "I am in business to develop leaders, and I make cabinets to pay the bills."

God has obviously distributed differing gifts to men. There are Servant Sams who are satisfied to run the same band saw in the same furniture plant for twenty years. Day after day they can stand there, do their job well, and go home each evening feeling fulfilled. And there are Production Pauls who wouldn't last more than a few days doing something like that. They would become frustrated with the monotony, think of faster ways to cut out the pieces, and mentally start designing new production lines. Within a short time they would be calculating the cost of production and the profit per unit, and probably pondering where they could obtain financing to buy out the operation. God has given us different gifts.

### "As It Hath Pleased Him"

The Apostle Paul uses the human body to illustrate the place for different gifts within the church. He writes about the foolishness of the eye saying to the hand, "I have no

> "I am in business to develop leaders, and I make cabinets to pay the bills."

need of thee."[a] What kind of body would we have if every member were an eye? "But now hath God set the members every one of them in the body, as it hath pleased him."[b] Paul isn't saying that every member of our body will be noticed equally. Rather, he is saying that each member has a specific function and gift, and these gifts have been given by God as it pleases Him. So what gifts have you been given? Should you be an employer or an employee, a David or an Andy?

Several years ago I met a small business owner named James. He had been in business for many years, and his financial life was in disarray. He kept slipping further into debt, and he wasn't sure why. There was plenty of demand for his business, but he just couldn't seem to make things work. As we sat down to talk, I couldn't help noticing the bookshelf behind him. Lots of books on the market are advertised to help you succeed in business, and James had many of them. As we talked, he mentioned various business seminars he had attended and advice he had received from different experts. I marveled as I listened. The books behind him were well worn. How could a man read all those books, listen to experts for years, and still have difficulty keeping money in the checkbook? The answer is simple. He was a Servant Sam trying to be a Production Paul, an ear attempting to be an eye. After years of struggle, James finally closed his business and is now happily working for someone else.

[a] 1 Corinthians 12:21
[b] 1 Corinthians 12:18

James lived in an area that promoted self-employment. "Real men have their own businesses" was the predominant philosophy, and men felt pressured to go on their own. I have watched this scenario play out in numerous communities, and when we pressure Servant Sams to become Larry Littles or Production Pauls, we create problems. The opposite is also true. If you teach that everyone should be content operating a band saw and that "real" followers of Jesus don't get involved in the business world, be prepared to find unfulfilled and restless men. Just as a tool works best when used for the task it was designed for, men function better when they utilize the gifts they were given.

## Who Am I?

How can I know what gifts God has given me? Should I be self-employed? While I don't know of any tests out there that will accurately answer this question, I believe there are some things you should consider.

- **Acknowledge the diversity of occupational gifts.** Understand that everyone has gifts, but no one has them all. A person given the patience to operate the same band saw year after year isn't less of a man than the owner of the factory. The band saw operator will have opportunities to reach out to fellow workers whom the owner cannot reach, and his daily life will be less cluttered. While the owner is cumbered with a multitude of daily pressing business decisions, the employee can concentrate on other things like praise, prayer, and service opportunities after work.

- **Ask for and listen to godly counsel.** I believe God takes pleasure in seeing His children enjoy their work, but enjoyment shouldn't be our only reference point. Just as ships use several points of reference when approaching a harbor, so should we in choosing an occupation. If you are married, what gifts does your spouse see in you? Or what about your local church? This is an excellent place to go for advice when brotherhood is working properly. You should have men around you who know your strengths and weaknesses, men who are able to bless you and hold you accountable.

- **It is an illusion to believe you must leave your occupation to be in full-time ministry.** God wants all of His servants to working for Him full-time. For some that may mean moving to a foreign country, and for others it may mean using business as a platform to take Jesus to the marketplace. Just as there are multiple occupations, so there are diverse needs to be filled in the Kingdom. If David or Andy had moved to China to minister to the Chinese, neither would have been able to reach out in the cabinet shop. What is important is not so much the place of ministry but the determination to minister, whether at home or abroad. Using our lives to further the Kingdom of Jesus Christ must be an intentional pursuit.

- **Recognize your obvious abilities.** Some can work well with their hands, and others are better suited to thinking through problems. What gifts have you been given? Aspiring to be a Production Paul while possessing few organizational skills will not work. A man attempting to lay bricks without having physical coordination will most likely starve. There should be visible fruit from the gifts you believe you have. In Exodus, when God called Bezaleel to oversee building the tabernacle, He listed Bezaleel's natural abilities. I think his gifts for designing and building were obvious to everyone. When he took gold to construct a candlestick, it looked like a candlestick when he was finished. If you believe you have been called to a certain occupation, there should be evidence of this calling in your life.

- **Occupational choices have a tremendous impact on home life.** You need to consider this as you contemplate your options. One older businessman shared his experience growing up on a farm. "We went out early each morning to milk and then returned to the house for breakfast and devotions. We spent time together discussing God's Word and then headed back out to work together." Today he sees fathers leaving home early in the morning, and he has concerns. "Our men have much more exposure to people than they used to, and this can be a blessing. But fathers must remember that they need to give more thought and energy to teaching than their parents did." In other words, where at one time learning happened more naturally because families spent more time together, fathers today need to be more intentional in teaching. Think about how a potential occupation will affect time with your spouse and children.

- **Work while you seek God's will.** When we are young, our talents are not always readily apparent. I have watched young men bounce from job to job, not sticking with any one trade because they don't believe it fits them. When the task becomes boring or difficult, they quit and go find something easier. They may assume that a job must always be enjoyable, and I've even heard some say, "This job just isn't me." It is fine to ponder what gifts God has given you, but be sure you are faithfully working while you ponder. Whatever the job, a time will come when it loses its original luster. Don't use the excuse of "seeking God's direction in my life" to avoid hard work. Be diligent even while you prayerfully consider your direction. You will learn much about your abilities by faithfully working even after the initial enjoyment is gone.

## Conclusion

Throughout the Bible we see God gifting men and calling them to specific tasks. Huram of Tyre, the man who created works of brass, is described like this: "And he was filled with wisdom, and understanding, and cunning to work all works in brass."[c] Maybe you think working in brass is of little consequence, but evidently God didn't. He called a particular man from a certain city to perform a specific task. Take Joseph and Daniel, whose skills in administration became known throughout the world. These men had certain gifts, and God was able to use them to further His cause.

Both employers and employees have an important place in the Kingdom of God. More important than what specific abilities God has given you is your willingness to use them for His glory. We need faithfulness in the workplace—men who are committed to doing their best with what God has given them. As Paul told the church at Colosse, "And whatsoever ye do, do it heartily, as to the Lord, and not unto men; knowing that of the Lord ye shall receive the reward of the inheritance: for ye serve the Lord Christ."[d]

[c] 1 Kings 7:14

[d] Colossians 3:23, 24

# *The Power of Perspective* 31

Many people don't like spiders. Some are even afraid of them. But few take such extreme measures to eliminate them as a man in the state of Washington. Firefighters responded to a call in West Seattle on July 15, 2014, to find a home completely engulfed in flames. The fire caused an estimated $60,000 in damage. When it was out and the smoke had cleared, the firemen inquired about the cause of the blaze.

The resident, whose name was not published, told investigators he had seen a spider in the laundry room of the rental house he lived in. He had tried to kill it, but the spider kept getting away and finally retreated into a small hole.

Desperate, he grabbed a lighter and an aerosol can of paint and created a makeshift blowtorch, aiming it at the hole where the spider had disappeared. Focused on eliminating the dreaded spider, he failed to notice that the wall had ignited.

Finally coming to his senses, the man tried to throw water on the fire, but the flames spread quickly into the attic and through the roof. "There were giant clouds of smoke just pouring out of the windows,"

a neighbor reported, and the man was forced to flee for his life.[1] The fire investigator reported, "He has to live with the fact that he set fire to the house he was living in," and then concluded by wryly adding that it was unlikely the spider survived the blaze.

## Perspective Is Everything

Most of us try to eliminate spiders in our homes. But this man became so focused on the spider that he forgot everything else. Fearful that the spider might escape, he briefly lost perspective, with drastic result.

When I stand back and try to summarize what Jesus taught about work, wealth, possessions, and business, the word perspective keeps coming to mind. Jesus never taught that a man shouldn't work hard, be involved in commerce, or operate a business. But all through His teachings, like an essential thread in a tapestry, He continually warned against losing perspective. He knows we need to live and earn income to survive. He knows a man needs food, shelter, and clothing, and He understands that someone needs to work to provide these. But He also understands our tendency to get so involved in providing for the temporal that we forget the eternal. We are capable, like the man determined to kill that spider, of forgetting things of much greater value while involved in business.

If you are going to successfully operate a business, no matter what it is, some things are essential. Bookkeeping is one of those things. If your business grows to any size at all, it is important to learn how to read a balance sheet, to understand what can be gained from a profit and loss report, and to grasp the value of cash flow. Yet as important as all this is, you must also remember that a day is coming when these things, which are so important now, will hold absolutely no value. Like the wrapper on a candy bar, they are useful for a while and then discarded. Jesus told parables, spoke sternly, and gave repeated warning about the danger of temporal things because we tend to lose perspective. The love of profit and wealth can change a man and gradually shift his overriding vision and mission.

## Vision Shift

Overriding goals can gradually change, and I can think of no better examples than some of our well-known institutions of higher education. Many of the premier universities in the United States started out with a clear vision but today have drifted far from their original purpose. Harvard University began with this profound mission statement: "Let every student be plainly instructed and earnestly pressed to consider well the main end of his life and studies is to know God and Jesus Christ which is eternal life."[2] What an amazing statement of vision! Notice the eternal perspective within the wording. The founders wanted that school to turn out graduates who knew God!

What happened? How could a school created for the express purpose of teaching individuals the importance of knowing God have drifted so far from its moorings? Harvard isn't just neglecting its original mission, it is going the opposite direction! But Harvard isn't alone. Just eighty years after Harvard was founded, New England pastors sensed that the college was drifting from its original vision. So they approached a wealthy philanthropist named Elihu Yale. Elihu agreed with their concern and provided funding. A new school, Yale University, was launched with a vision for reclaiming the spiritual vision they saw Harvard losing. Yet today both universities are considered secular and don't even pretend to teach their students to know God. How did these institutions lose their original vision?

If you trace the vision shift in many universities, you will discover money as one of the root problems. Operating a large university is expensive and fundraising is a constant pursuit. When a wealthy donor speaks, a university tends to listen. One man who changed higher education was Andrew Carnegie.[3] Having a massive amount of wealth and believing in the power of education, Carnegie gave millions of dollars to institutions of higher education. But he applied parameters to his giving. In his Letter of Gift, he clearly stipulated that schools under a religious governance structure or that require students to adhere to a statement of belief would be excluded from his foundation's grants.[4] You can imagine the discussions around university board tables. Additional funding was hard to find, and competition with other universities was fierce. They started imagining what that extra funding could do. All they had to do was make some changes to the vision and purpose of their school.

Consequently, teaching men to know God, the very reason these schools had been founded, got lost. Just a little money, and they lost their reason for existing. They went from teaching students that nothing is more important than serving God to challenging His existence and teaching humanistic ideology. They lost their eternal perspective.

## The Allure of the Temporal

Maintaining an eternal perspective in our culture is difficult. Recently I read an article telling about a $100-million house built by a celebrity. The article described how huge the house was, reported the cost of the furniture, and showed pictures of its elaborate landscaping, pool, and extravagant waterfalls. While reading I was suddenly hit by some soul-searching questions. "Why am I interested in this article? Why do I find a $100-million home fascinating?" The sobering end of that little time of self-examination was this: I am still enamored with wealth and what it can do. I have written books on its dangers and warned against it in seminars, but the reality is I still struggle with giving earthly wealth a higher value than it deserves.

If that house is like every other house I am familiar with, it has already begun to disintegrate. The paint has started to fade, concrete has cracked, and the roof has begun to deteriorate. Unless someone actively maintains it, within one hundred years it will be completely worthless. From an eternal perspective, that structure has little value. In my head I understand all this. But something inside me still wants to ascribe great value to a $100-million house. I have trouble maintaining proper perspective regarding earthly wealth.

Production is another area where most businessmen struggle with perspective. For some this can be even more captivating than the money it brings. Recently I visited a small manufacturing plant. The owner took me through the plant, starting in the receiving area and ending up where the final product was on display. Along the way, he told me how each department added value to the original material. There is something exciting about seeing raw material, something of little value, gradually transformed into a useful product.

Businessmen love this process, and I have talked with many who have ended up with a large business, not because they love money, but because they love the process of production. Whether they are involved in farming, construction, manufacturing, or providing some kind of service, they enjoy efficiency and what it can accomplish. They love taking on the next challenge, and for many this path leads to larger businesses than they ever envisioned. But remember, God placed that inner drive for efficiency and production in us for a reason. And unless we identify and pursue that reason, we will arrive at the end of life and look back with deep regret. Production

> **Production without purpose is worthless.**

without purpose is worthless. Production is only of value when held in proper perspective.

### Proper Perspective

The local people had never seen anything like it. They walked along the beach with friends and family, searching for shells or anything else the sea had washed up on the sand. Good shells were hard to find, and early in the morning before others ventured out was the best time to search. But on this morning, December 26, 2004, something very unusual occurred. The sea suddenly receded a half mile farther than normal, exposing a huge area of previously unexposed sand. What an unprecedented beachcombing break! Never before had this much beach been exposed, and never

had the opportunity for finding beautiful shells been greater. Giddy tourists ran out onto this vast expanse, laughing and taking advantage of this once-in-a-lifetime chance. Locals ran out as well. It was an amazing opportunity!

This rare phenomenon lasted for just ten minutes. Suddenly everything changed, and people looking out to sea froze in horror. A fifty-foot wall of water barreled down upon them, bringing an abrupt end to their joy and their lives. The massive tsunami destroyed everything in its path, and an estimated 169,000 people along the northwest side of Banda Aceh, Indonesia, were killed.[5] Roughly one-third of the city was flattened, with only an occasional tree or chunk of concrete surviving the incredible power of the tsunami.

For just a little while the huge expanse of beach had looked like a beachcomber's dream. Never in anyone's memory had there ever been such a chance to find rare, beautiful seashells. But what appeared to be a wonderful opportunity was actually a horrific deathtrap. For just ten minutes, people along that beach had a choice. Some used those few minutes to seek lovely shells. But the few who were truly wise used those minutes to seek higher ground.

We live in an unprecedented time. If you have been blessed with the gift of business administration, you are surrounded with business possibilities. And if you are in America, you live in a country known around the world as the land of opportunity. The millions of people constantly trying to enter this country force the government to use fences and guards. A man who comes to America, works hard, and saves money can eventually become financially independent. Many of us have been blessed by the business climate and opportunity here.

But there are some sobering similarities between America and the final ten minutes at Banda Aceh. Imagine that you had been there on the beach. Whether or not those last ten minutes were a good beachcombing opportunity depended entirely on your perspective. In the short-term it was an unparalleled chance to gather shells. But from a long-term perspective, the cost of focusing on shells was disastrous. We are living in a time of tremendous business opportunity. But I want to encourage you to look at these opportunities from an eternal perspective. If you find your life consumed with expanding your company, accumulating wealth, and seeking out more business opportunities, it is time for you to seek higher ground!

## Eternal Perspective

If you follow Jesus, you are a pilgrim here on earth. Pilgrims go through an area, but they travel lightly. In many ways they live like everyone else. But there is a major difference. Their affection is somewhere else. A pilgrim is going somewhere, and he doesn't put his roots down any deeper than he needs to as he travels.

So what does this mean for the Christian businessman? It means everything he does is done with an eye on the Kingdom of God. It may affect how large his business grows. A time may come when he says, "That's enough. I know I could get larger, but in light of the goal, I am choosing not to." Or he may see the need for employment and resources within the Kingdom and decide to expand. But there is one thing a Kingdom pilgrim perspective will never do. It will not cause a man to see resources as something to be used for excessive personal consumption.

Recently a financially successful businessman told me, "Choosing to live frugally while having plenty isn't easy. I could take much more home for my personal use, but I choose not to. I could purchase a boat for the weekends, but I choose not to. The more God gives me, the more responsible I feel, and it gives me an urgency to not waste resources, and to do all I can to be a faithful steward."

Another shared the burden he feels for his more than one hundred employees as they watch his standard of living. "It is a challenge to put frugality into shoe leather. But a practical way of living speaks to my men and tells them what I am actually living for." It is a rare man who owns a large business while still trying to live as a pilgrim.

Whether you are dealing with employees, a difficult customer, or strategic business planning, make your daily decisions and chart your course from an eternal perspective. It is the only perspective worth having. We live in a rapidly changing world. In our great-grandparents' day, filing bankruptcy was cause for shame, and a lawyer who specialized in divorce would have starved. But those days are over. Perhaps more than ever before we need men, whether employers or employees, with integrity and a purposeful focus on the Kingdom of God.

Does earthly wealth still intrigue you? Do you find yourself enamored with the temporal? Do you at times question whether trying to swim against an ungodly value system is worth it? If so, there is a man in the Bible who identified with your struggle. Asaph the psalm writer found himself envying the ungodly and becoming jealous of the wealthy. He wondered why everything seemed to go so well for those blaspheming the name of the Lord and ignoring His Word. But Asaph said he struggled with these thoughts only until he went into the sanctuary of God and came to understand their end."[a] What changed in the sanctuary? He saw God! And when a man sees God for who He really is and juxtaposes God's values with his own, it has a drastic impact on his perspective!

If you continually struggle to maintain a proper perspective in business, you may need to abandon your career. Jesus called for extreme measures when dealing with distractions, regardless of the cost. If there are situations that call for removal of a right hand or an eye,[b] surely a vocational change isn't out of the question. All of us will struggle at times to keep perspective. When this occurs, go back and analyze your connection with God. Getting close to God will always change a man.

### Wanted: Transformed Businessmen

We need men today like Moses. He could have had anything he desired, but he walked away from earthly wealth and power, and chose to live his life to the glory of God. We need men who, like the Apostle Paul, throw all their energy into the God's Kingdom and count everything else "but loss for the excellency of the knowledge of Christ Jesus."[c] Today we need more transformed men who have been called by God to serve Him in the marketplace—men who use commerce as a platform to display the glory and superiority of the Kingdom of God. Paul had this aspiration for the church at Philippi. It was his desire that they interact within their culture "without rebuke, in the midst of a crooked and perverse nation, among whom ye shine as lights in the world."[d] That is still God's will for us today.

---

[a] Psalm 73:17
[b] Matthew 5:29, 30
[c] Philippians 3:8
[d] Philippians 2:15

## Conclusion

I don't know what kind of business paradigm you operate under or how much thought you have given to using your business as a mission. Maybe you have assumed giving a portion of your profit is really all God is looking for. But I want to challenge you to aim higher. Use the marketplace to demonstrate something greater. Intentionally put your occupation on the altar and let the power of the Lord Jesus control your decisions. Not only will you impact unbelievers, but other Christians will be inspired to examine their foundational reasons for being in business.

There is a mission field right where you are, and Jesus is looking for those who will trust Him and surrender their will when making daily decisions in business. So go forth in His power. Remember, it's not your business, but the Lord's. Purpose to use His teachings as your primary reference point. Resolve to make decisions from His perspective. If you do so, your occupational life will provide a public demonstration of what the whole world of commerce could be like if every businessman were a follower of Jesus Christ!

# Endnotes

## Introduction
[1] Vinh Chung, *Where the Wind Leads,* Thomas Nelson Publishers, Nashville, TN, 2014.
[2] Ibid, p. 341.
[3] Ibid, p. 342.
[4] Anup Shah, "Poverty facts and stats," *Global Issues,* <http://www.globalissues.org/article/26/poverty-facts-and-stats>, accessed on September 5, 2014.

## Chapter One
[1] George MacDonald, *Thomas Wingfold, Curate,* edited and reprinted by Michael Phillips as *The Curate's Awakening,* Bethany House Publishers, Minneapolis, MN, 1985, pg. 146.

## Chapter Five
[1] United Nations Development Programme, "Despite high unemployment, young Nicaraguans are hopeful," December 7, 2011, <http://www.undp.org/content/undp/en/home/presscenter/articles/2011/12/07/-informe-nacional-de-desarrollo-humano-2011-las-juventudes-construyendo-nicaragua-/>, accessed on May 6, 2014.
[2] Mary Bellis, "The Invention of VELCRO," <http://inventors.about.com/library/weekly/aa091297.htm>, accessed on May 7, 2014.

## Chapter Six
[1] Greg Mortenson and David Oliver Relin, *Three Cups of Tea,* Penguin Books, London, 2006.
[2] Jon Krakauer, "Is It Time to Forgive Greg Mortenson?" *The Daily Beast,* April 8, 2013, <http://www.thedailybeast.com/articles/2013/04/08/is-it-time-to-forgive-greg-mortenson.html>, accessed on May 9, 2014.
[3] "Obama gives Nobel money to charity," *Associated Press,* March 11, 2010, <http://www.nbcnews.com/id/35823326/ns/us_news-giving/t/obama-gives-nobel-money-charity/>, accessed on May 12, 2014.
[4] Jon Krakauer, *Three Cups of Deceit,* Byliner Press, San Francisco, 2011.
[5] Leslie Kaufman, "David Oliver Relin, Adventurous Journalist, Dies at 49," *The*

*New York Times,* December 2, 2012, <http://www.nytimes.com/2012/12/03/business/media/david-oliver-relin-co-author-of-three-cups-of-tea-dies-at-49.html?_r=0>, accessed on May 12, 2014.

## Chapter Seven
[1] World Vision, <http://www.wvartists.org/artist-detail/175127/joel-osteen/>, accessed on June 5, 2014.
[2] William Lee Miller, *Arguing About Slavery: The Great Battle in the United States Congress,* Vintage Books, New York, 1996, p. 139.
[3] Marci A. Hamilton, *God vs. the Gavel,* Cambridge University Press, Cambridge, NY, 2005, p. 60.
[4] Norman H. Baynes (ed.), Hitler's Speeches, April 1922–August 1939, Vol. 1, Oxford University Press, 1942, pp. 19–20.

## Chapter Eight
[1] The Lampo Group, Inc., "About Dave," <http://www.daveramsey.com/company/about-dave/>, accessed on May 13, 2014.

## Chapter Eleven
[1] "Colorado baker to stop making wedding cakes after losing discrimination case," *CBS News,* May 31, 2014, <http://www.cbsnews.com/news/colorado-baker-to-stop-making-wedding-cakes-after-losing-discrimination-case/>, accessed on June 9, 2014.

## Chapter Twelve
[1] Philip Schaff (ed.), "Reply to Faustus," *The Nicene and Post-Nicene Fathers,* series 1, Vol. 4, p. 301.

## Chapter Thirteen
[1] A.W. Tozer, *The Pursuit of God,* Christian Publications Inc., Harrisburg, PA, 1948, p. 119.

## Chapter Fourteen
[1] Justin Martyr, *The Ante-Nicene Fathers,* Eerdmans Publishing Company, Grand Rapids, Michigan, reprinted 1989, p. 244.

## Chapter Fifteen
[1] Academy of Achievement, "Rosa Parks Biography -- Academy of Achievement," last modified February 26, 2010, <http://www.achievement.org/autodoc/page/ell0bio-1>, accessed on June 30, 2014.
[2] Brian Warner, "Larry Ellison Net Worth," <http://www.celebritynetworth.com/richest-businessmen/ceos/larry-ellison-net-worth/>, accessed on June 30, 2014.
[3] Catholic Online, "St. Simeon the Stylite," <http://www.catholic.org/saints/saint.php?saint_id=5616>, accessed on June 30, 2014.
[4] Herbert Thurston, "St. Simeon Stylites the Elder," *The Catholic Encyclopedia,* Vol. 13, Robert Appleton Company, New York, 1912, <http://www.newadvent.org/cathen/13795a.htm>, accessed on June 30, 2014.

## Chapter Sixteen

[1] Bob Greene, "A final toast for the Doolittle Raiders," CNN, April 14, 2013, <http://www.cnn.com/2013/04/14/opinion/greene-doolittle-raiders/index.html?eref=mrss_igoogle_cnn>, accessed on July 1, 2014.

## Chapter Seventeen

[1] Hobby Lobby, <http://www.hobbylobby.com/our_company/>, accessed on July 1, 2014.

[2] Jonathan Merritt, "Stop calling Hobby Lobby a Christian business," *The Week,* June 17, 2014, <http://theweek.com/article/index/263225/stop-calling-hobby-lobby-a-christian-business#axzz34uWgDyYE>, accessed on July 1, 2014.

[3] Hobby Lobby, <http://www.hobbylobby.com/our_company/>, accessed on July 1, 2014.

[4] Leslie Marshall, "Hobby Lobby's Hypocrisy," *U.S. News & World Report,* March 26, 2014, <http://www.usnews.com/opinion/leslie-marshall/2014/03/26/hobby-lobbys-china-hypocrisy>, accessed on July 1, 2014.

[5] Eric Wesner, *Success Made Simple,* Jossey-Bass Publishers, San Francisco, 2010, p. x.

[6] Ibid., p. 83.

[7] Glenn Rifkin, "The Amish Flock From Farms to Small Businesses," *The New York Times,* January 7, 2009, <http://www.nytimes.com/2009/01/08/business/smallbusiness/08sbiz.html?pagewanted=all&_r=0>, accessed on July 2, 2014.

## Chapter Eighteen

[1] Brian Edwards, *God's Outlaw: The Story of William Tyndale and the English Bible,* Evangelical Press, Darlington, England, 1976.

## Chapter Nineteen

[1] Larry Burkett, *Business by the Book,* Thomas Nelson Publishers, Nashville, TN, 1998, p. 3.

[2] Business Coaching, <http://www.businesscoaching.com/business-coaching-statistics/>, accessed on July 7, 2014.

## Chapter Twenty

[1] Michael Bergdahl, *The Ten Rules of Sam Walton,* John Wiley & Sons, Hoboken, New Jersey, 2006, p. 193.

## Chapter Twenty-One

[1] Jerome Paine Bates, *The World's Highway to Fortune, Happiness, and Heaven,* J. Fairbanks & Co., Chicago, 1880, p. 213.

## Chapter Twenty-Two

[1] Peter B. Grazier, "The Miracle of Pittron Steel," October 1, 1997, <http://teambuildersplus.com/articles/miracle-pittron-steel>, accessed on August 12, 2104.

## Chapter Twenty-Three

[1] Art Swift, "Honesty and Ethics Rating of Clergy Slides to New Low," <http://www.gallup.com/poll/166298/honesty-ethics-rating-clergy-slides-new-low.aspx>, accessed on July 9, 2014.

[2] "Domino's tough love on itself is getting noticed," *Associated Press,* January 11, 2010, <http://www.nbcnews.com/id/34812047/ns/business-us_business/t/dominos-tough-love-itself-getting-noticed/>, accessed on July 9, 2014.

[3] Anna Louise Jackson et al., "Domino's 'Brutally Honest' Ads Offset Slow Consumer Spending," *Bloomberg Business,* October 17, 2011, <http://www.bloomberg.com/news/2011-10-17/domino-s-brutally-honest-ads-offset-slowing-consumer-spending.html>, accessed on July 9, 2014.

[4] Sue Unerman and Jonathan Salem Baskin, *Tell the Truth: Honesty Is Your Most Powerful Marketing Tool,* BenBella Books, Dallas, TX, 2012, Introduction.

[5] Lisa Earle McLeod, *Selling With Noble Purpose,* John Wiley & Sons Inc., Hoboken, NJ, 2013, Introduction.

[6] Herbert Hoover, <http://thoughts.forbes.com/thoughts/honesty-herbert-hoover-no-public-man>, accessed on July 10, 2014.

## Chapter Twenty-Four

[1] Dunn & Bradstreet Update, "Why is business credit important to my business?" <https://iupdate.dnb.com/iUpdate/whyBusinessCredit.htm>, accessed on July 10, 2014.

[2] Matt Krantz, "26 U.S. companies with no long-term debt," May 29, 2014, <http://americasmarkets.usatoday.com/2014/05/29/debt-free-26-u-s-companies-shun-debt/>, accessed on July 10, 2014.

## Chapter Twenty-Six

[1] "The Pastor of Hermas," Book Third, Similitude Fourth, *The Ante-Nicene Fathers,* Vol. 2, Eerdmans Publishing Company, reprinted 1989, p. 33.

## Chapter Twenty-Seven

[1] Dr. Henry Cloud, *Necessary Endings,* HarperCollins Publishers, New York, 2010, p. 23.

## Chapter Twenty-Eight

[1] Joe Maxwell, "The Mission of Business," *Christianity Today,* November 9, 2007, <http://www.christianitytoday.com/ct/2007/november/24.24.html?paging=off>, accessed on July 18, 2014.

[2] Chris Mitchell, "Christian Pioneer Ken Crowell's Life Celebrated," *CBN News,* February 3, 2012, <http://www.cbn.com/cbnnews/insideisrael/2012/January/Israelis-Say-Goodbye-to-Ken-Crowell-Business-Pioneer-/>, accessed on July 18, 2014.

[3] Andy Newman, "Their Mission: Spreading the Word Through Business," *The New York Times,* November 14, 2005, <http://www.nytimes.com/2005/11/14/giving/14newman.html?pagewanted=all&_r=2&>, accessed on July 21, 2014.

[4] Patrick Lai, *Tentmaking: Business as Missions,* Authentic Media, Waynesboro, GA, 2005, p. 42.

## Chapter Twenty-Nine

[1] BBC News, <http://news.bbc.co.uk/2/hi/business/3398913.stm>, accessed on July 21, 2014.

[2] Dennis I. Dickstein and Robert H. Flast, *No Excuses: A Business Approach to Managing Operational Risk,* John Wiley & Sons, Hoboken, NJ, 2009, p. 82.

## Chapter Thirty-One

[1] Victoria Cavaliere, "Washington state man tries to kill spider with blowtorch, sets house ablaze," <http://us.mobile.reuters.com/article/oddlyEnoughNews/idUSKBN-0FL2V020140716>, accessed July 22, 2104.

[2] All About History, "History of Harvard," <http://www.allabouthistory.org/history-of-harvard.htm>, accessed on July 23, 2014.

[3] Peter Greer and Chris Horst, *Mission Drift,* Bethany House Publishers, Bloomington, MN, 2014, p. 113.

[4] "Carnegie Millions for College Pension Fund," *The New York Times,* April 28, 1905.

[5] Barry Bearak, "The Day the Sea Came," *The New York Times,* November 27, 2005, <http://query.nytimes.com/gst/fullpage.html?res=9D01E2D71F3EF934A-15752C1A9639C8B63&pagewanted=1>, accessed on June 23, 2015.

# *About the Author*

Gary Miller was raised in an Anabaptist community in California and today lives with his wife Patty and family in the Pacific Northwest. Gary desires to encourage Christians in developed countries to share their resources and focus more on the Kingdom of God. He also continues to work with the poor in developing countries and directs the SALT Microfinance Solutions program for Christian Aid Ministries. This program offers business and spiritual teaching to those living in chronic poverty, provides small loans, and assists them in learning how to use their God-given resources to become sustainable.

Gary's enthusiasm for Kingdom building has prompted him to write the Kingdom-Focused Living series. *It's Not Your Business* is his fifth book in the series. He also continues to write teaching manuals for developing countries. See page 247 for a list of his published works.

Have you been inspired by Gary's materials? Maybe you have questions, or perhaps you even disagree with the author. Share your thoughts by sending an e-mail to kingdomfinance@camoh.org or writing to Christian Aid Ministries, P.O. Box 360, Berlin, Ohio 44610.

# Additional Resources
## by Gary Miller

### Life in a Global Village

Would your worldview change if the world population were shrunk to a village of one hundred people and you lived in that village? Full-color book.

### Small Business Handbook

A manual used in microfinance programs in developing countries. Includes devotionals and practical business teaching. Ideal for missions and churches.

### Following Jesus in Everyday Life

A teaching manual ideal for mission settings. Each lesson addresses a Biblical principle and includes a story and discussion questions. Black and white illustrations.

### A Good Soldier of Jesus Christ

A teaching manual like *Following Jesus in Everyday Life*, but targeting youth.

---

## Audio books

*Kingdom-Focused Finances for the Family, Charting a Course in Your Youth, Going Till You're Gone, The Other Side of the Wall,* and *Life in a Global Village.*

---

## Audio and PowerPoint seminars

### Kingdom-Focused Finances Seminar—3 audio CDs

This three-session seminar takes you beyond our culture's view of money and possessions, and challenges you to examine your heart by looking at your treasure.

### Kingdom-Focused Finances Seminar Audio PowerPoint—3 CDs

With the visual aid included on these CDs, you can now follow along on the slides Gary uses in his seminars while you listen to the presentation. A good tool for group study or individual use. A computer is needed to view these CDs.

---

## Audio and PowerPoint presentation

### Life in a Global Village

# The Way to God and Peace

We live in a world contaminated by sin. Sin is anything that goes against God's holy standards. When we do not follow the guidelines that God our Creator gave us, we are guilty of sin. Sin separates us from God, the source of life.

Since the time when the first man and woman, Adam and Eve, sinned in the Garden of Eden, sin has been universal. The Bible says that we all have "sinned and come short of the glory of God" (Romans 3:23). It also says that the natural consequence for that sin is eternal death, or punishment in an eternal hell: "Then when lust hath conceived, it bringeth forth sin: and sin, when it is finished, bringeth forth death" (James 1:15).

But we do not have to suffer eternal death in hell. God provided forgiveness for our sins through the death of His only Son, Jesus Christ. Because Jesus was perfect and without sin, He could die in our place. "For God so loved the world that he gave his only begotten Son, that whosoever believeth in him should not perish, but have everlasting life" (John 3:16).

A sacrifice is something given to benefit someone else. It costs the giver greatly. Jesus was God's sacrifice. Jesus' death takes away the penalty of sin for everyone who accepts this sacrifice and truly repents of their sins. To repent of sins means to be truly sorry for and turn away from the things we have done that have violated God's standards. (Acts 2:38; 3:19).

Jesus died, but He did not remain dead. After three days, God's

Spirit miraculously raised Him to life again. God's Spirit does something similar in us. When we receive Jesus as our sacrifice and repent of our sins, our hearts are changed. We become spiritually alive! We develop new desires and attitudes (2 Corinthians 5:17). We begin to make choices that please God (1 John 3:9). If we do fail and commit sins, we can ask God for forgiveness. "If we confess our sins, he is faithful and just to forgive us our sins, and to cleanse us from all unrighteousness" (1 John 1:9).

Once our hearts have been changed, we want to continue growing spiritually. We will be happy to let Jesus be the Master of our lives and will want to become more like Him. To do this, we must meditate on God's Word and commune with God in prayer. We will testify to others of this change by being baptized and sharing the good news of God's victory over sin and death. Fellowship with a faithful group of believers will strengthen our walk with God (1 John 1:7).